LESSONS FROM THE MASTER

Visit our web site at
www.albahouse.org
(for orders www.stpauls.us)

or call 1-800-343-2522 (ALBA)
and request current catalog

Lessons from the Master

Living Like Jesus

Alex Basile

ST PAULS

Library of Congress Cataloging-in-Publication Data

Basile, Alex.
  Lessons from the Master: living like Jesus / by Alex Basile.
    p. cm.
  ISBN-13: 978-0-8189-1295-5
  ISBN-10: 0-8189-1295-2
  1. Jesus Christ—Teachings. 2. Catholic teenagers—Religious life. I. Title.
  BS2415.B37 2009
  232.9'54—dc22
                        2009009497

Produced and designed in the United States of America by the
Fathers and Brothers of the Society of St. Paul,
2187 Victory Boulevard, Staten Island, New York 10314-6603
as part of their communications apostolate.

ISBN 10: 0-8189-1295-2
ISBN 13: 978-0-8189-1295-5

Printing Information:

Current Printing - first digit   1   2   3   4   5   6   7   8   9   10

Year of Current Printing - first year shown

2009   2010   2011   2012   2013   2014   2015   2016   2017   2018

Table of Contents

Preface

❦

Our Marianist Educational Tradition often emphasizes the fact that "atmosphere educates." Schools, universities, Christian homes, religious education centers, parishes are called to create atmospheres of faith. It is not just about choosing the right books and a good curriculum. We are all responsible for creating Christ-centered atmospheres where people can grow. How has atmosphere touched the life of Alex Basile?

When I first read Alex's *Lessons from the Master: Living like Jesus* I began to ask myself.... Why did he choose the image of Jesus as Master? This in turn prompted me to make some personal connections.

When you enter Kellenberg Memorial, where Alex serves in so many capacities, the lobby has a mosaic of "Jesus the Teacher" created from many different types of wood. Alex passes this mosaic many times each day. So I ask myself this question. How does this mosaic of "Jesus the Teacher" influence Alex? I would venture to say that this book is a mosaic not of wood but of the many teaching moments in the life of Jesus woven together as lessons on how we can find meaning in our life with Christ. The book is a mosaic of the lessons of Jesus who teaches about forgiveness and fidelity, truth and consequences, chastity and charity, and more besides.

Alex introduces each chapter with a mosaic of insightful quotations from ordinary life where we listen to both popes and presidents, poets and priests, philosophers and psychologists, all of whom inspire us to take the Christ challenge of conversion and growth. These then are linked to our own life experiences, the experiences of Alex and finally to the life experience of Jesus, the Master.

We all need teachers. We all need individuals who will point us in the right direction especially when we experience personal darkness or confusion. Jesus gives us a mosaic of opportunity from which to learn. I invite you to follow Alex and let him be your mentor as you look to Jesus, the Master, in hope.

Father Thomas A. Cardone, S.M.

Acknowledgments

To my loving wife, Allison,
and my beautiful children, Alex and Maggie,
for your daily inspiration.
You show me the face of Christ everyday.

To my parents, Al and Eileen,
for the foundation of faith that carries me through all things.

To Christine Phillips
for your professional guidance and patience.

To Bridget, George, Rose, Bridget and Emily
for your gifts of love and laughter.

To Jeff Harris
for rising to every challenge and constant friendship.

To my Uncle Don
for sharing your love of our Church.

This book is dedicated to my friend and mentor,
Father Thomas Cardone.
You teach me something new every day.

Introduction

After I graduated college, God blessed me with an incredible opportunity to own my own business. I had worked at our neighborhood delicatessen since my senior year in high school. Not having the funds to pay for the deli myself, my parents took a second mortgage on their house. Suddenly, I became an entrepreneur. I owned the deli for twelve years. During the last year of owning the deli, I was married and I realized that the demands of the business would hinder my responsibilities as a husband and someday, as a father. So I decided to sell the deli. As I tried to sell the store, I put together my resume. I met with a career counselor who told me that I should highlight my years in the food and beverage business. He promised me that people would be impressed by my dedication and work ethic exhibited by the many hours each week that I poured into my business. So with my resume in hand, I ventured into the next chapter of my life.

In the early 1990's the Coca Cola Bottling Company had restructured their business. This corporate shake-up would increase the demand for sales representatives and my business contacts said I was a perfect fit for their company. The thought of working for an ever expanding corporation excited me. To sell "The Real Thing," as the advertisements stated, would have endless possibilities. The deli business taught me to be a natural salesman. I loved interacting with people and this seemed like the most logical job for me.

One day a regular customer, Ed, asked me about my plans after the sale of the deli. I told him about my possibilities. Ed worked as a teacher. He had started in high school and now taught on the college level. Ed wondered if I had ever thought about teaching as a career. He knew that I had spent every Wednesday teaching CCD in my parish. "I want to see you in front of the classroom someday," he begged. Ed was a very soft spoken gentleman, but when he spoke, I listened. Our conversations were always simple, but Ed left me with his pearls of wisdom. It was clear to anyone who met him that Ed loved his faith. He never preached. He just glowed as an example of Jesus in everything he did.

I pondered Ed's proposition. "Could I be a successful teacher?" I asked myself. Teaching religion seemed to be the most natural subject for me, as I had twelve years of experience. I loved my faith and enjoyed spending each Wednesday with the kids in my class. Suddenly, selling "The Real Thing" took on a whole new meaning. The only thing that people needed to possess was Jesus. He is The Real Thing. His disciples referred to Jesus as the Master. People came to Jesus for real answers to life's real questions. I had the opportunity to talk about Jesus every day. The choice became an easy one and I have been in the classroom ever since. I have been given the privilege of teaching young people the key to life — Jesus. Selling The Real Thing took on a whole new meaning thanks to Ed. I thank God for Ed's wisdom every day.

The Invitation

*If every call to Christ and His righteousness
is a call to suffering, the converse is equally true —
every call to suffering is a call to Christ,
a promotion, an invitation to come up higher.*

Charles Bent

Matthew sat at his customs post when Jesus approached him. Peter and Andrew had just arrived back on shore when He pushed them out for another fishing expedition. The rich young man came to Jesus filled with confidence, but walked away disappointed when the Master asked him to become a disciple. We see it over and over again in the Gospels. Jesus invited people to follow Him. Sometimes they accepted His invitation, sometimes they refused. Discipleship began with an invitation from the Master. Jesus now extends His invitation to us. True discipleship calls us to emulate Jesus as well as follow Him. Jesus asked His followers to come and sit by His side and listen to His stories. He knew about the challenges of life. When His friend Martha chastised her sister for sitting at the feet of Jesus while she served their guests

1

by herself, Jesus reprimanded Martha for criticizing her sister. He praised Mary for her willingness to spend time with Him. Jesus has a message for each one of us. To learn from Him, we must tune out the distractions around us and make an appointment to spend time with the Master.

As Jesus taught, He told His disciples the parable of the sower and the seed. Jesus explained that the seed will grow only if the soil is properly prepared. Our hearts must be open to hear the words of Jesus. We must be willing to put His message into action, to take on the attributes of the perfect One. He lived so we may live, here and in His kingdom. Learn from Him and life will make sense. As citizens of the 21st century, we have grown accustomed to a quick-fix world. The channels on our televisions are flooded with infomercials that try to satisfy our every need. We search for answers: How can I find happiness? How will I know what to do as my life unfolds? We somehow fool ourselves into thinking that we can go it alone without any help. C.S. Lewis said, "Self-sufficiency is the enemy of salvation." Without the help that God provides, our lives will seem empty. We must put our trust in Jesus. He is everything we need:

> I am the true vine, and My Father is the vinedresser. Every branch in Me that does not bear fruit, He takes away; and every branch that bears fruit, He prunes so that it may bear more fruit. You are already clean because of the word which I have spoken to you. Abide in Me, and I in you. As the branch cannot bear fruit of itself unless it abides in the vine, so neither can you unless you abide in Me. I am the vine, you are the branches; he who abides in Me and I in him, he bears much fruit, for apart from Me you can do nothing.
> (John 15:1-5)

We are all connected through the love of Christ. With Him in our lives, we will never walk alone. For the Christian, the answer is simple: Look to Jesus Christ! Our goal should be to know Jesus and imitate Him. The slogan "What would Jesus do?" has become the mantra for Christian living. In every circumstance, in any situation, we need to ask ourselves: How would Jesus handle this situation? The Gospels give us a clear guide for living. Even though we live more than two thousand years after He walked this earth as a man, we need to look no further than the Scriptures to see the pattern of all proper behavior. Jesus showed us how to live happily. We must respond positively to His invitation. Allow Him into your life. Let Christ permeate your very being. As St. Paul says:

> Let the word of Christ dwell in you richly, as in all wisdom you teach and admonish one another, singing psalms, hymns, and spiritual songs with gratitude in your hearts to God. And whatever you do, in word or in deed, do everything in the name of the Lord Jesus, giving thanks to God the Father through Him.
> (Colossians 3:16-17)

The 19th century artist William Holman Hunt painted "The Light of the World." The painting depicts Jesus standing at a door poised to knock. The pathway on which He walks to the door has overgrown because of the lack of use. Although Jesus looks to enter the house, there is no handle on the outside of the door. When people viewed the painting, they assumed that Hunt had forgotten to paint the doorknob. But Hunt wanted to convey the message that the door to Christ can only be opened from the inside. We must be ready to greet Jesus. We can only know Him if we are willing to meet Him face to face. He constantly seeks us. Our receptiveness to Him can open the door. This is a free will decision. No one can respond for us.

Learn what He taught. Seek His wisdom. Include Him in every aspect of your life. Your life will be complete and you will change for the better. Your days will be fulfilled. Love Him as He loves you. Open the door and invite Him into your heart.

Turn the Other Cheek

The glory of Christianity is to conquer by forgiveness.

William Blake

The residents of Jerusalem gossiped like many people do today. The rumors had buzzed around the town for months. Finally, she was caught in the act. How could she do such a thing? Sleeping with a married man was unthinkable. This sin was punishable by death. That's exactly what the citizens of Jerusalem had in mind that day. The angry mob chased the woman with stones clenched in their hands. They wanted the punishment to fit the crime. Public executions exhibited the brutality of the times. Public stoning involved the common man. People literally took the law into their own hands.

They not only saw this woman as a problem, they feared Jesus as well. The Jewish leaders would use the adulterous woman in their plot to trap Him. So the mob brought the woman to Jesus who spent most of His days with sinners like this woman. If He forgave her sins, He would be teaching in contradiction to Mosaic Law. They posed their angry question: "Now in the law, Moses

5

commanded us to stone such a woman. So what do you say?" When Jesus turned their question back on them to make the crowd examine their own lives, they walked away. He was concerned about forgiveness and our consciousness of our own spiritual lives. Jesus knew that reconciling our relationships was at the heart of our path to God. God's unending love and outstretched arms are always available to us. He wanted our arms to be unconditionally outstretched to those around us. This message was central to the ministry of Jesus.

On the day Jesus died, He left us with an example of forgiveness that we could never ignore. During His trial, the soldiers used the plight of Jesus for their own amusement. The original plan of Pilate was to torture Jesus and release Him. He wanted to teach Jesus a lesson and show the Sanhedrin that he meant business. Then Pilate, coerced to crucify the Nazorean, handed Him over to be killed. On His journey to Calvary the soldiers and crowd continued to mock Jesus. They spat upon Him as He passed. Even those who once followed Him showed their disgust and betrayal. The deafening blows of the hammer signaled that He was one step closer to death. As He was raised on the cross, the onlookers continued to taunt the Master: "If you are truly God, then save yourself!" Jesus uttered not a word of disdain for His persecutors; rather He called on His Father to forgive those who had done the unthinkable. "Father, forgive them for they know not what they do," He cried from the cross. "Why would He forgive them?" I have often thought. These people deserved the wrath of God, not His forgiveness. But that's not how God works. His unconditional love endured the nails, the thorns and the scourging. Hatred and resentment are washed away by the blood of the Lamb. God's love transcends all our human failings. He understands relationships better than anyone. He knows the difficulties that arise between people. Grudges and resentment only drag us down. He shows us that forgiveness is the answer. Forgiveness makes everything new again.

We spend too much time worrying about what others are doing. With our eyes transfixed on our televisions, we are fascinated by the lives of celebrities. Gossip buzzes through the hallways of our schools, our faculty rooms, our PTA meetings, and our business lunches. We hesitate to forgive. We would rather enjoy the misery of others than to extend a hand of friendship and love. Jesus reminded us that we should be thinking differently:

> Stop judging others and you will not be judged. Stop condemning and you will not be condemned. Forgive and you will be forgiven.... Why do you notice the splinter in your brother's eye, but do not perceive the wooden beam in your own? ... You hypocrite! Remove the wooden beam from your eye first; then you will see clearly to remove the splinter in your brother's eye.
>
> (Luke 7:37-42)

Jesus offered sound advice to us: Stop focusing on the faults of your brother or sister and look within yourself. Change begins with the individual. Push aside your self-centeredness and think about others. The hesitation to forgive others, is keeping you from having true interpersonal relationships. Resentment is a burden far too heavy to carry. Happiness will be impossible to find if we do not make peace with those who hurt and disappoint us. Showing others mercy is the only path to having our own faults forgiven. C.S. Lewis said,

> We find that the work of forgiveness has to be done over and over again. We forgive, we mortify our re-

sentment; a week later some chain of thought carries us back to the original offense and we discover the old resentment blazing away as if nothing had been done about it at all. We need to forgive our brother seventy times seven not only for 490 offenses but for one offense.

We need to make forgiveness an everyday practice. The more we forgive, the easier it will become. It must become part of our everyday life. People will disappoint us every day; we must be able to forgive every day. Forgiveness helps us put our lives in order and move on to another day.

If you want some practical reasons for forgiveness in your life, look no further then to what the medical journals have to say about the benefits of forgiveness. *The Harvard Women's Health Watch* (January 2005) outlined the benefits of granting forgiveness to someone who may have wronged you:

Forgiveness reduces stress. Nursing a grudge can place serious strains on your body: Muscles remain tense. Blood pressure becomes elevated. There is an increase in sweating. Forgiveness has been proven to improve heart rate. You may have stronger relationships. A recent study found that women who were able to forgive their spouses and feel kindhearted toward them, resolved conflicts more effectively. People with chronic back pain had less pain and anxiety when they practiced meditation focusing on converting anger to compassion. By forgiving another person, you make yourself, not the person who may have hurt you — responsible for your happiness. People who talk about forgiveness during psychotherapy experience greater improvements than people who don't discuss forgiveness, said one survey.

Have you ever thought about the phrase "forgive and forget"? We cannot pretend that reality does not happen. We do not forget that someone is addicted to drugs or that a spouse has been unfaithful. Ignoring the wrong does not solve the problem. But the ability to forgive strengthens us as humans. Forgiveness brings us closer to Jesus Christ.

Each year, many people visit the Amish in Pennsylvania. Lancaster County has become one of the most popular travel destinations in America. The Amish are known for their simple, Christian approach to living and their gracious hospitality. In 2006, Charles Carl Roberts ambushed an Amish school house in West Nickel Mines and murdered five young girls. As the local residents tried to cope with their grief, members of the press waited to hear the response of the Amish to this terrible tragedy. They interviewed Rita Rhoads who was present for the birth of two of the five murdered girls. She said, "If you have Jesus in your heart and He has forgiven you, how can you not forgive other people?" If we live as Jesus did and imitate Him, we can find forgiving others an easier task than if we had to forgive on our own.

Listen to His words from the cross and think about those who have hurt and betrayed you. If Jesus can utter those words of forgiveness, can't you? Let the words, "I forgive you," lift your heavy heart and ease your own burdens. Forgiving others allows us to look into the eyes of the Master Himself as we ask Him to forgive us our trespasses. Forgive and your world will change immediately for the better.

The Outstretched Hand

The body is a house of many windows;
there we all sit, showing ourselves and crying out
to the passers-by to come and love us.

Robert Louis Stevenson

People looked down on Zacchaeus in more ways than one. Even though he was small in stature, most of the residents of Jericho knew him well. Zacchaeus was the chief tax collector in Jericho. People despised the tax collectors. They collected money for the Romans and skimmed much for themselves. Their conspiracy with the Romans symbolized the oppression of the times. Zacchaeus was one of the richest people in Jericho. He thought he had it all. In reality, life left him poor in so many other ways. Zacchaeus was aware of the reputation of Jesus. His popularity attracted Zacchaeus to see Him that day. By coming to see Jesus, his life would change forever. Zacchaeus could not see above the crowd, so he climbed a sycamore tree to get a better look at the Master.

When he reached the place, Jesus looked up and said to him, "Zacchaeus, come down quickly, for today I must stay at your house." And he came down quickly and received Him with joy. When they saw this, they began to grumble, saying, "He has gone to stay at the house of a sinner." But Zacchaeus stood there and said to the Lord, "Behold, half of my possessions, Lord, I shall give to the poor and if I have extorted anything from anyone I shall repay it four times over."

(Luke 19:5-8)

People were angry with Jesus for choosing to dine with a sinner. Zacchaeus was an outcast. The people of Jericho avoided him like the plague. But if you knew Jesus, you realized that He didn't seek out the popular and accepted. He spent His time with the lonely and forgotten. He gravitated to the person that others avoided. You hear it over and over in the Gospels, "Why is Jesus with *that* person?" Jesus wants us to know that neither looks nor popularity nor being accepted by the crowd make any difference. He desires to be with us. He shows us that love and companionship can change people. Jesus surrounded Himself with the unpopular. Even His disciples shook their heads in disbelief when He ate with prostitutes and other sinners. Jesus reminded the apostles that those who were well did not need the help of a doctor, only those who were sick.

But what made these people sin in the first place? What brought them into despair? Their selfishness isolated themselves from God and others. Jesus drew them back into the fold. He helped them remember that they belonged to God's kingdom where everyone was equal. The presence of Jesus in their lives led to conversion. They changed after Jesus accepted them. As human beings, we were not created to be alone. We want to be in communion with others. The International Theological Commission explained our need for communion in this way:

> Human beings, created in the image of God, are persons called to enjoy communion and to exercise stewardship in a physical universe. The activities entailed by interpersonal communion and responsible stewardship engage the spiritual — intellectual and affective — capacities of human persons, but they do not leave the body behind. Human beings are physical beings sharing a world with other physical beings. Implicit in the Catholic theology of the imago Dei is the profound truth that the material world creates the conditions for the engagement of human persons with one another. (July 2004)

Jesus knew the situations in our classrooms, our cafeterias, our companies, and our towns. We label people as early as grammar school: the geeks, the jocks, the freaks, the in-crowd. We do not hesitate to compartmentalize others. Unfortunately, these labels can stay with people forever. These names can cause isolation. Jesus knew that there are people who sit alone and unloved. These are the people whom we walk past and fail to engage in conversation. We ignore them because we do not want to be inconvenienced. We neglect to invite them into our cliques. We hesitate to move out of our comfortable circles and engage them. We worry about what others may think, or perhaps, we are too selfish to give our time to another. They remain isolated. They pretend to be apathetic and not mind eating alone. They look uninterested as they read a book to pass the time. They have become accustomed to eating in restaurants alone. But inside, loneliness tears them apart.

As Jesus gave the conditions for entering the kingdom of heaven, He didn't read a checklist of sins to avoid; rather He asked us to treat each person we meet as if he or she were Jesus, Himself. Mother Teresa takes the teaching of Jesus one step further.

> When Christ said: "I was hungry and you fed me," He didn't mean only the hunger for food and for drink; He also meant the hunger to be loved. Jesus Himself experienced His loneliness. He came amongst His own and His own received Him not, and it hurt Him then and it has kept on hurting Him, the same hunger, the same loneliness, the same having no one to be accepted by and to be loved and wanted by. Every human being in that case resembles Christ in His loneliness and that is the hardest part, that's real hunger.

As Christians we are called to satisfy the hunger of our fellow neighbor to be loved. People are mistaken when they think they can exist by themselves. Without love and companionship we will be miserable. He urged us to be the hand that reaches out to the person in need. Jesus knew that our lives are busy. He realized that our choice to engage the outcast may leave our popularity in question. There are so many people who want to be included. They ache inside to be accepted. She waits for an invitation on a Friday night. He prays that someone would ask him to join them for lunch. They have become accustomed to spending time alone, but they are only fooling themselves. They have no other choice.

Jesus surrounded Himself with outcasts. He recognized the unloved and gave them a place at His table. He makes no excuses for the inclusion of the unwanted. His love and friendship made people feel alive. Being locked in the cocoon of isolation can prevent a person from discovering his or her role in the body of Christ. They are all around us. Open your eyes and look for them. If we are to follow His example, we can't worry about how others may judge us. Jesus certainly didn't care.

Pope John Paul urged us to seek out the lonely:

> There in the midst of humankind, is the dwelling of Christ, who asks you to dry every tear in His name and to remind whoever feels lonely that no one whose hope is placed in Him is ever alone.

Be the loving hand that extends to the outcast. As you do, you may hear the sighs of disgust. Give the outcast a place at your table. Invite them to your party. Talk to them in the cafeteria. Start a conversation in the office. Engage them on the checkout line in the supermarket. Make a difference in someone's life. You may see people shaking their heads in disbelief. You may hear her exclaim, "Can you believe they are talking to *them*!" Just remember, you are keeping company with Christ. A simple gesture may totally change a person's life. There are so many hearts waiting to be touched. He wants you to act as His hands. The words of St. Teresa of Avila's prayer remind us of our obligation:

> Christ has no body now but yours; no hands, no feet on earth but yours; yours are the eyes through which He looks with compassion on this world. Christ has no body now on earth but yours.

Open your social circle to the unwanted and unpopular. As the Master showed His apostles the importance of moving out of their comfort zones, make your friends realize that no one should be left alone. Have the courage to reach out to those who have been neglected by others. More people will admire you, rather than criticize you. Change a life with a kind word and an invitation. Pull someone out of the clouds of isolation. Be the outstretched hand of Christ.

The Faithful Son

To maintain a joyful family requires much from both the parents and the children. Each member of the family has to become, in a special way, the servant of the others.

Pope John Paul II

Everyone loves a wedding. Great music, splendid cuisine and, of course, a full bar. Imagine, if while you were dancing, the music stopped. When they served dinner, they ran out of prime rib or salmon. As you sauntered up to the bar, the bartender told you, there was nothing left to drink. At a wedding, the food, music and drink should flow freely. You don't skimp at this kind of celebration. Everyone involved in a wedding celebration desperately wants to create the perfect day. This is not realistic. Even Mary at Cana knew this from her experience when they ran out of wine. Imagine the waiters saying, "How could we run out of wine? What do we do now?" Mary watched and saw the crisis unfold. She did not hesitate to call upon her Son for help. Unlike the rest of the guests, Mary knew who He was: the King of Kings, God of All. He could do anything. She knew the magnitude of the plea.

His ministry had not begun, but she needed Him now. If the wine had truly run dry, the host would surely be humiliated.

Jesus said to her, "Woman, how does your concern affect me? My hour has not yet come." Mary did not waver in her concern. She directed the servers, "Do whatever He tells you." The quick exchange between mother and Son has been examined by biblical scholars for centuries, but one thing is clear: even though Jesus states His feelings strongly, He would never disappoint His mother. Jesus constantly prompts us to think beyond our earthly existence, but He never overlooks His human relationships. And so be it, He obeyed the request of His mother and began His mission at Cana. Jesus recognized Mary's role in the plan of salvation. With obedience, He followed her will because He saw in it the will of His Heavenly Father.

As children, we find ourselves at odds with our parents from infancy. I recall being at dinner with my wife, our two-year-old son Alex and our six-month-old daughter Maggie. Alex, feeling neglected because of the attention we were giving to Maggie, started to act up at the restaurant. We had taken him to restaurants since he was three weeks old. We had traveled with him to Italy and Ireland. He was a well-behaved and easy-going child. As he fidgeted in his high-chair, I leaned over to him and sternly told him, "Stop!" As I went back to talking to my wife, Alex hurled a piece of bread that bounced off of my forehead. Stunned, I sat there speechless. Luckily, my wife interceded and young Joe Frazier was quickly removed from the table before I realized what had happened.

We resent being told what to do and how to act. We can all recall a story when we argued with our parents. The most difficult years between a parent and child usually occur when the child enters the depths of the teenage world. The teenager can't imagine how their parents could understand what they are going through. We fail to recognize the wisdom of our parents. This sentiment does not disappear simply because we emerge from adolescence. During our teenage years we think our parents are the dumbest people on the planet only to realize that we were the ones who needed to learn some things about life. We eventually grow to appreciate the wisdom of our parents. What can we learn from Jesus when it comes to parent/child relationships? We don't have many instances where Jesus interacts with His parents, but we see Him show them the respect they deserve. Throughout the life of Jesus, we could have seen Him respond, "What do they know? They are just human." He always kept in mind His role as a child. Pope John Paul II spoke about the child Jesus in a general audience address on December 4, 1996:

> The Gospel of Luke, particularly attentive to the childhood period, says that at Nazareth Jesus was obedient to Joseph and Mary (Luke 2:51). This dependence shows us that Jesus was receptive, open to the teaching of His mother and Joseph, who also carried out their task by virtue of the docility He constantly showed.

Because Joseph is not present during the ministry of Jesus and, of course, the crucifixion, we assume that he died before Jesus began His public life. Jesus spent at least twenty-five years in Nazareth working as a carpenter and caring for His mother. He shines as an example of love and holiness as He fulfills His earthly duties. Even in the ordinary things of life, He shows us perfection. We take the Fourth Commandment for granted as a straightforward edict, but how do we properly "honor our mother and father"? Do we show them the respect they deserve? Do we take their love and generosity for granted? Do we take more than we give?

I don't think I understood what my parents had done for me until I became a father myself. The first month with a newborn baby can shock anyone into reality. Around-the-clock feedings and diaper changes make you appreciate even a few hours of uninterrupted sleep. The nights I spent in the wee hours feeding my children as newborns gave me time to reflect on my parents' love. I worry when my children are ill. I pray that they grow to be healthy and happy. Parents watch their children grow only to give them the freedom to "fly on their own."

As we reflect on our relationships with our parents, we must place ourselves in the shoes of Jesus and focus on His life in Nazareth. Imagine the Master humbling Himself as a son. He lived a simple existence focusing on the care of His family. The love of His parents led to the extension of the love He showed for all of humanity. His time in Nazareth was essential. The obedience He demonstrated towards Mary and Joseph would be transformed in Gethsemane and on the road to Calvary.

Our parents aren't perfect, but neither are we. They have given us the beautiful gift of life. Take time to recognize the wisdom that they have attained through life experience. Don't dismiss their advice without first thinking about their own life experience. Cherish the time that you have together. They will not be around forever. Enjoy the simple, ordinary moments. Shut off the television and listen to the stories that show you a glimpse into your family history. Look into their eyes and recognize the profound love that they have shared with you. Appreciate your parents as Jesus appreciated Mary and Joseph. They have shared your time in Bethlehem, your adolescence in Nazareth, your moments at Cana, and they are with you as you carry your cross. Love and cherish them always.

The Eye of the Needle

All earthly joy begins pleasantly,
but at the end it gnaws and kills.

Thomas à Kempis

My father was born in 1931. Two years earlier, the Stock Market had crashed and America began its worst economic time in history. When my father speaks about growing up, he rarely refers to this chapter of his life as the Great Depression. His parents, Italian immigrants, struggled to make ends meet. When you speak to him about his childhood, he fondly remembers the simplicity of those days. Most meals consisted of pasta and a simple vegetable. His father, a plasterer and mason, found employment through President Franklin Roosevelt's work programs. These programs created jobs for many Americans who were unemployed due to the desolate economy. My father learned to get by in life with the bare minimum, yet he never considered himself poor.

As I grew up, my father taught me that the flashiness of our culture was just an illusion. When I bought my first car, he stood in the showroom of the dealership looking at the cost of the cars and shook his head. Growing up in a different time, I didn't understand his hesitation. I worked hard for a living and felt that if I wanted to spend my money on something I wanted, I shouldn't feel guilty about it. You would often hear him say, "You don't need that!" If something needed to be repaired around our house, he repaired it himself. He could go to the fanciest Italian restaurant and order chicken Parmesan and be happy. He focused, instead, on the gathering of family and friends rather than the status of the restaurant or the cost of the meal.

Many people who followed Jesus heard Him speak about the kingdom. They wanted to know how to attain eternal life. A rich young man stood before Jesus and looked for answers. He considered himself a good person. He told Jesus that he obeyed the commandments and followed the law. But Jesus knew obstacles stood in the way of the kingdom. The young man loved his earthly possessions. Perhaps, he loved his riches more than God. Jesus told him to go and sell what he possessed, give the money to the poor, and then come back and follow Him. The young man sadly walked away for he could not give away his material things. Jesus said:

> Amen I say to you, it will be hard for one who is rich to enter the kingdom of heaven. Again I say to you, it is easier for a camel to pass through the eye of a needle than for one who is rich to enter the kingdom of God.   (Matthew 19:23-24)

Jesus knew well about our attachment to our "toys." He pushed the rich young man to rid himself of the obstacles that kept him from being in communion with God. Life is about choices and we can't have two masters. We must be willing to sacrifice temporary joys for eternal happiness.

The poverty of Jesus is evident in the Gospels. Born amidst animals in the stable, He came into this world penniless. His mother wrapped her newborn Child with a cloth and laid Him in the manger. This cloth was His only possession. His earthly existence ended with His mother receiving His body from the cross and covering Him in a cloth for burial. The life of Jesus reminds us that we enter this world with nothing and leave with nothing. Material possessions are worthless.

We are groomed from the earliest age to achieve good grades in school. We believe that these grades will get us into a good college and this in turn will lead us to a successful and lucrative career. Somewhere along the journey we forget to pick a career that will fulfill us. I know too many people who dread going to work each day. We trade the big paycheck for happiness. All of this is great in the eyes of the world, but is it great in the eyes of God?

We are privileged to live in the most prosperous country in the world at the most technologically advanced time in history. All of our needs are fulfilled by the latest inventions. We depend on our devices to help us stay in touch with our friends and family. We trade in our computers for quicker models with more memory. We buy cell phones with sleeker designs and updated features. Our car seems inadequate when the newest model is unveiled. We buy into the philosophy that "newer is better." In an ever changing technological world, we find ourselves on a treadmill that never stops revolving. As long as a new product is on the horizon, we will have the desire to buy it.

How does the pursuit of these objects affect our relationships with God and others? Do we spend more time worrying about what we want instead of what we need to do to help those around us? On his pilgrimage to the United States in 1979, Pope John Paul II addressed a group of students:

> Materialistic concerns and one-sided values are never sufficient to fill the heart and mind of a human person. A life reduced to the sole dimension of possessions, of consumer goods, of temporal concerns will never let you discover and enjoy the richness of your humanity. It is only through God in Jesus, God made man, that you will fully understand what you are. He will unveil to you the true greatness of yourselves: that you are redeemed by Him and taken up in His love; that you are made truly free in Him who said about Himself, "If the Son frees you, you will be freed indeed." (John 8:36)

As Jesus challenged the rich young man, He hoped that he would take a step forward into the kingdom rather than to fall back into the security of his possessions. He wanted him to realize that money only offers us a temporary escape from life. Permanent joy is found in Jesus. He provides the foundation for true happiness. We can strike it rich by surrendering to Christ.

We need to take inventory of our lives. We need to determine the things that give us meaning. Do we put more hope and faith in the things we own, rather than in the people we love? Our material possessions will not bring us eternal happiness; a relationship with Jesus will. Stop chasing the empty dreams of wealth. Material possessions weigh us down. The image of the "eye of the needle" urges us to trim our excess baggage so we may fly to Him. Remember both the earth's richest and poorest citizens will stand penniless before the Lord at the final judgment. Thomas Merton said, "The tighter you squeeze, the less you have." Let go of your earthly things and embrace the people in your life. Hold on to God with all your might. Learn from the rich young man. Do not turn your back and walk away from Jesus. Instead, follow Him. He has extended an invitation to you. Investing in Jesus the Master will bear riches beyond this life. Invest in Him. The dividends are endless.

LESSON

A Be-attitude

Humor is the great thing, the saving thing.
The minute it crops up, all our irritation and resentments
slip away, and a sunny spirit takes their place.

Mark Twain

Each year the freshman class watches the film *Jesus of Nazareth* during several assemblies as part of their Scripture course. Franco Zeffirelli who is famous for his version of *Romeo and Juliet* brought the Scripture to life in this epic film. Zeffirelli's masterpiece is several hours long as it tells the story of Jesus from birth to resurrection. Zeffirelli chose Robert Powell to portray Jesus. His piercing blue eyes and stoic English delivery made this Jesus seem aloof. In the movie, Jesus seems above the ordinary happenings around Him. Through the entire movie Powell barely cracks a smile. When we talk about the movie in class, the most frequent comment is: "Jesus seems so serious." I have often pondered this question: Would the Incarnate God, the God who made us, have a sense of humor? The only logical answer to this question is, "Yes!" When God created us in His own image He gave humans the ability to think, to reason, to love and yes, to laugh. The heart of Jesus' mission focuses on our need to be happy. He desires us to lead fulfilled lives. Following Jesus gives us joy and laughter, an expression of that inner joy.

Just as Jesus preached in the Beatitudes, He too must have discovered the joys of humanity through His Incarnation. Hundreds, even thousands of people, flocked to hear Him speak. People pushed their way through crowds to get a better glimpse of Him. Even the places at dinner were argued over. A person this popular must have beamed with joy. His bright smile and lilting voice would win over even the most skeptical listener. People flocked to Him because of His loving message and His engaging charisma. The real Jesus invited people to follow Him not only with His words, but with His welcoming eyes. We assume that a man with such a serious message must have had a serious demeanor as well. If Jesus was such a "downer," He would have stood on a street corner preaching His Gospel and been ignored. Even the apostles never would have followed Him. His mission would have ended with an empty boat on the shore of the Sea of Galilee. Jesus practiced what He preached. The Beatitudes invite us to join Him in a deep state of joy and happiness.

As we grow older, life grows more complex. The average adult laughs very little compared to the average six year old. When I listen to my daughter Maggie (age 7) play, she laughs so often it becomes contagious. As Jesus implored us to become like little children, I wonder if He wanted us to laugh more. Jesus needed a sense of humor to disarm the angry. I wouldn't doubt if He even poked fun at Himself at times, thus disempowering those who waged constant battles against Him. Jesus would have gone insane dealing with those hypocrites daily without a sense of humor.

Jesus never apologized for being who He was. Jesus bore

the truth of His being in everything He did. He realized that the major obstacle to being happy is coming to terms with who we are. Father John Powell in his book, *Why Am I Afraid to Tell You Who I Am?* reminds us that fully human people are comfortable with their physical, psychological, and spiritual attributes. They accept themselves as good people. Jesus wants us to look in the mirror and like what we see. He loves when we can laugh at our faults and overlook our limitations. He loves the uniqueness of our creation. Happiness begins and ends with Christ. Because He is part of us, it also begins with ourselves. We have control over our ability to be happy. Turn up the radio in the car and sing at the top of your lungs. Stop looking at the glass as half empty and realize that it is half full instead. Don't allow a low moment or bad experience to ruin your day. Jesus wants us to have perspective. Turn the channel to a show that will make your sides split. Wake up each day to the words of Mark Twain:

> Sing like no one's listening, love like you've never been hurt, dance like nobody's watching, and live like it's heaven on earth.

The presence of Jesus on earth helps us to see that we are not alone in our darkest moments. Jesus defeated gloom with laughter.

Many great speakers start a speech with a memorable story or a clever joke. What about Jesus? Do you think He had any good opening lines? I do. Make no mistake, Jesus loved to laugh and smile. Indeed the Incarnation does not make sense without laughter. Those who sat at a table with Jesus had the pleasure of listening to the One who created humor tell the funniest jokes and stories ever written. Maybe the Gospel writers assumed that we would know such a fact. Simply because the New Testament didn't end up as a collection as His best one-liners does not mean that we should overlook the importance of a sense of humor as a reflection of Jesus Christ. Eternal happiness begins in the life we live right now.

If Jesus asked me to edit the Beatitudes, I think He would chuckle at my addition: Blessed are they who seek holiness through humor, for they will be able to handle any life situation. Listen to the Master and stop taking life so seriously. Smile!

#

The Body Beautiful

Chastity is the cement of civilization and progress.
Without it there is no stability in society,
and without it one cannot attain the Science of Life.

Mary Baker Eddy

For an unmarried person, the greatest years of independence and growth occur in the post college years. Starting a new career and enjoying the company of friends are usually the only responsibilities of the twenty-something. At twenty-one years old, I bought the deli that I worked in during high school and college. Spending countless hours in the store, I looked to relax with friends after the deli closed at night. We found a great place in Bayside, Queens called "The Minstrel Boy," an Irish pub and restaurant that featured the music of Carl Corcoran and Larry Austin. Our group enjoyed many nights in this bar. Bars with music seemed to attract a different crowd. The clientele of the Minstrel Boy appreciated good music and the atmosphere of the pub. The Minstrel Boy was a great place to meet people. My friends and I dated many girls that we met there. Socialization is what the twenties are all about. The person going through the dating process must discern between finding the person you want to marry and moving from one relationship to another.

Starting at the advent of puberty, the challenge of every person is understanding and controlling sexual desire. If our society promotes the notion "If it feels good, do it!" where does a person learn how to live with these desires? We must first make the distinction between sex and love. When two people "hooked-up" at the bar, love was usually the last thing on their minds. There are many degrees of an encounter in a bar. For some the initial introduction led to a first date. For others this conversation brought about an embrace or a kiss. Then for others it went beyond. What made a person give themselves sexually to, basically, a stranger? We all have known guys and girls who were considered "easy." We saw them use each chance encounter as an opportunity to "hook-up." What were they looking for? How many times can they be hurt before they realized that these relationships always ended the same way? Author Erich Fromm described this sense of desperation as "separateness." It is our fear of not being accepted for who we are. We dread the thought of being lonely, so we are willing to do anything to avoid it. Loneliness can cause people to do desperate things. Separateness produces an inner anxiety. Fromm, in *The Art of Loving*, explains:

> The awareness of human separation, without reunion by love — is the source of shame. It is at the same time the source of guilt and anxiety. The deepest need of man, then, is the need to overcome his separateness, to leave the prison of his aloneness.

Using sex to overcome loneliness is a mistake. Fromm explains:

It becomes a desperate attempt to escape the anxiety engendered by separateness, and it results in an ever-increasing sense of separateness, since the sexual act without love never bridges the gap between two human beings, except momentarily.

As we watch our favorite TV shows and movies, we are not surprised to see people involved in casual relationships having sex during a first date. Our culture has minimized the importance of sex. Sex has become another one of life's pleasures that may be enjoyed on any whim. Sex serves as recreation rather than the sacred communion it was meant to be between two people who love each other deeply.

When the best selling book *The DaVinci Code* claimed that Jesus married Mary Magdalene, many lifelong Christians actually believed that it could be true. "Why wouldn't He have been married?" They ask, "He was human!" Every time a man and woman interact, unfortunately, we believe that sexual tension must exist. We assume simply because Jesus had sexual desire, He must have had sexual relationships. We often forget that Jesus encountered the devil before He began His earthly mission. Satan offered Him the riches and pleasures of the world if He would abandon His Father's plan. Jesus rebuffed his temptation.

Our society condones giving in to our urges. It promotes lust as a normal component of the human condition and allows us to act on any urge that may arise. When lust overcomes us, our culture presumes that the only course of action is to submit to the temptation. Jesus understood sexuality as the path to true communion. As the Creator, He gave us this gift to become one with another. He realized that lust degraded another to a mere object.

Through His incarnation, Jesus personified chastity. Chastity elevates the human heart and allows us to seek purity in our lives. Pope John Paul II defined the Church's teaching on sexuality in his teaching on human sexuality called the Theology of the Body. He presented his teaching from 1979 to 1984 during his weekly addresses. In them, John Paul tells us:

> Jesus completely overturns the external, ritual system of purity. Nothing from the outside can make a man pure or impure, he says — only what is in his heart. The bodily aspects of our sexuality do not make a person "dirty." And no ritual bath, by itself, can make a person pure. According to Jesus, purity is a matter of the heart.

Christopher West has traveled around the world bringing Pope John Paul II's message to Christians. In his eloquent book, *The Good News about Sex and Marriage,* he says:

> Chastity is not primarily a "no" to illicit sex. Chastity is first and foremost a great "yes" to the meaning of sex, to the goodness of being created as male and female in the image of God. Chastity isn't repressive. It's totally liberating. It frees us from the tendency to use others for selfish gratification and enables us to love others as Christ loves us. The virtue of chastity is therefore essential if we are to discover and fulfill the very meaning of our being and existence.

When lust captures the heart, another person becomes a mere possession. We value them no more than as a means to our sexual release. Jesus calls us to lift the weight of our sin and restore our hearts to the fullness of love. He wants us to embrace our sexuality, not deny it. Where love exists, purity can prevail. Our selfishness fuels the fire of lust.

Invite God into your relationships. Treat all people as you would Jesus, even those with whom you are sexually attracted. Replacing unfettered sexual desire with mature love allows us to see each other as we are created to be: children of God. Imagine the person to whom you are attracted as your own son or daughter. How would you want someone to treat them? Certainly not as an object. We need to realize that society distorts the beauty of sexuality and hopes to lure us into its trap. As true disciples of Christ, we need to fight this battle daily. Living a life of chastity requires us to make sacrifices. We must resist the temptation to indulge in the momentary emptiness of the sexual fling and ask God for the strength to live His love in all we do.

Jesus was a great lover; He was a lover of chastity. He exhibits this through the sacredness of His single life. His chastity shines in the way He treats the women in His life. The Master showed us that a life of purity is possible. He replaced the feelings of lust with true genuine love and communion. Look at His life as a way to take our passions and transform them into love for others.

Follow the Leader

❦

If your actions inspire others to dream more, learn more,
do more and become more, you are a leader.

John Quincy Adams

As a senior in high school, my history teacher asked our class to research our family history. At the time, I knew a little about my mother's family. We had traveled to Ireland a couple of times and visited the places where my ancestors lived. My maternal great-grandparents raised livestock in Ireland. During our visits, our cousins entertained my family and we had the pleasure of experiencing the land of my grandparents first-hand. The history of my father's family, though, was still a mystery.

My grandfather had died several years earlier so I set up a time when I could interview my grandmother. We spoke for hours about my grandfather's life in Italy. He was a native of San Giacomo, a small town in the Calabria region of Italy. His father raised sheep in the hills of San Giacomo. They grew up poor and life was extremely difficult. Working as a shepherd held little promise for the future, so my grandfather left Italy for

New York. Shepherds were the poorest of the poor. They spent endless hours in their fields tending to their sheep. It was not a glamorous life, but it was a peaceful one. On my trips to Ireland, we would often see a shepherd wandering the fields gathering up his flock after a day of grazing. He would summon his sheep with a distinct whistle or call. They recognized his voice and they ran to him. I often wondered what it was like for my grandfather as he wandered the hills of Calabria tending his sheep. The heat of the summer scorched the grass on the hills. He must have come home exhausted after a long day in the sun.

Jesus knew the life of the shepherd well. He used this image when He spoke of Himself:

> "Very truly, I tell you, anyone who does not enter the sheepfold by the gate but climbs in by another way is a thief and a bandit. The one who enters by the gate is the shepherd of the sheep. The gatekeeper opens the gate for him, and the sheep hear his voice. He calls his own sheep by name and leads them out. When he has brought out all his own, he goes ahead of them, and the sheep follow him because they know his voice. They will not follow a stranger, but they will run from him because they do not know the voice of strangers." Jesus used this figure of speech with them, but they did not understand what He was saying to them. So again Jesus said to them, "Very truly, I tell you, I am the gate for the sheep. All who came before Me are thieves and bandits; but the sheep did not listen to them. I am the gate. Whoever enters by Me will be saved, and will come in and go out and find pasture. The thief comes only to steal and kill and destroy. I came that they may have life, and have it abundantly."   (John 10:1-10)

Jesus knew His audience needed spiritual leadership. As the shepherd, He would lead His flock to eternal happiness.

He understands that we will be lost if we journey on our own. As our leader, He provides the direction that we require. He nourishes our souls and shows us the path to heaven. The image of the Good Shepherd symbolizes the personal and loving relationship that Jesus has with us, His flock. As His disciples, how can we become shepherds ourselves? Within our own social circles, we can provide spiritual leadership to those who need it.

1. Set the moral standards for those around you. As St. Francis said, "Preach the Gospel and use words only when necessary." Actions *do* speak louder than words and people notice how we act. Jesus encourages us to be an individual in communion rather than someone in a herd who neither thinks nor reflects.

2. Be the person who stops gossip before it spreads. Gossip tears down others in order to build up ourselves. Jealousy and envy stem from insecurity. People who ride the rumor train are usually unhappy with themselves. Make sure people understand the truth and put an end to harmful chatter.

3. Becoming people who live the Gospel through our actions gives others a first hand experience of Christ. In the age of herd conformity, people need a moral voice. They need a voice that differentiates right from wrong.

4. Bring Christ to every situation and circumstance. At the party on Saturday night, on the baseball field, or sitting having a quiet moment with friends, make Jesus present to others. We must set the moral example for our friends and members of our families.

5. We act as shepherds as we nourish those around us with the Gospel message. It is not necessary to recite chapter and verse from the Bible; rather, live as an example of Jesus Christ.

6. Cultivate the goodness of this world and extinguish evil as it breeds. When good people are silent, evil triumphs. If you see something, say something. Call people out on their improper behavior.

7. Help others encounter Jesus through patience, kindness, and forgiveness. At the office or at school, in the cashier line or on the highway, we can become spiritual leaders. We can provide a road to heaven for others, as Jesus does for us.

8. Share your faith with others and help them discover the living God. You do not have to become a sidewalk preacher to bring Christ to others. Introduce the people around you to prayer. Initiate saying grace before meals. A gentle reminder of God's presence can go a long way.

Invite friends and other family members to attend church with you. Some people do not go to Mass, simply because they have never been asked.

The Good Shepherd protects His flock. As shepherds, it is our responsibility to protect ourselves and others from the poisons of the culture of death. Our society endorses indulging in sex and materialism as the path to true happiness. Called to holiness, we find fulfillment in the beauty of our relationship with God. We can create our own culture and shield ourselves from the frenzy that this world has to offer. A shepherd must be aware of wolves. Wolves attack the flock because they are threatened by their association with Jesus. Protect yourself and others with the truth of Christ. Stand tall and others will follow. Shine as His example in the world. Be a beacon that provides light for those in the darkness. Share the inner peace that Christ brings to you with others.

In his book *Mere Christianity,* C.S. Lewis describes the dilemma facing the Christian each day:

> The real problem of the Christian life comes where people do not usually look for it. It comes the very moment you wake up each morning. All of your wishes and hopes for the day rush at you like wild animals. And the first job each morning consists simply in shoving them all back; in listening to that other voice; taking that other point of view, letting that other larger, stronger, quieter life come flowing in. And so on, all day. Standing back from all your natural fussings and frettings; coming out of the wind.
> (*Mere Christianity* Book IV, Chapter 8)

Be the voice of the Good Shepherd. Call others and ask them to follow. Look for those who have gone astray. Remember no one should be left behind. Help others to push away the craziness of the world and hear what really matters. He needs you to be a leader in your own flock. They wait for your direction. Bring them home. Show them the way.

9

The Whole Truth

Having a clear faith, based on the creed of the Church
is often labeled today as fundamentalism. Whereas relativism,
which is letting oneself be tossed and swept along
by every wind of teaching, look like the only attitude
acceptable to today's standards.

Pope Benedict XVI

In 1969, the New York Mets stunned the baseball world and defeated the Baltimore Orioles to become the World Champions of Baseball. As a six year old, I watched the magic unfold and baseball became my passion. During baseball season, I torture my poor wife with the Mets game de jour. At a young age, my son Alex caught baseball fever. He became not only a Mets fan, but a fan of the sport of baseball. He studies how each player holds the bat and how each pitcher stands as they throw the ball. He has learned the rules of baseball and appreciates the way the game is played.

As a teacher, I have the luxury of spending each July and August in Breezy Point, Queens. Of course, baseball games are a part of our daily routine. Recently, we played a game and some of Alex's beach friends joined us. Alex and I were on one team and his two friends were on the other. I pitched to Matthew and he grounded to me. I threw the ball to Alex at first base for an out. Matthew, still at home plate, yelled "Foul!" Alex threw up his arms in disbelief. "How could a ground ball to the pitcher be foul?", he exclaimed. He charged from first base like a warrior into battle. "You're out Matthew, let the next batter hit," he pleaded. Matthew stood his ground. "If you're going to cheat, I'm not going to play," he said, as he stormed off the field. Alex shook his head and muttered to himself, "He just doesn't understand the rules!" Alex wondered why his friend couldn't comprehend one of the simplest rules of baseball. You must hit the ball between the lines in order for it to count. Unfortunately, Matthew is a product of the sports world that we have created for our kids. I have sat at Little League games where a child is at bat for ten minutes because he is unable to hit the ball. We fear hurting a child's feelings by saying, "Three strikes and you are out; you'll do better next time." In some leagues every child that plays gets a trophy simply for playing the game.

The father of one of my students would call me, as a guidance counselor, after his daughter failed making the team for which she tried out. After nine consecutive seasons where she did not make a team, her father called me more furious than ever. He claimed that our coaches were un-Christian. When I suggested that his daughter may not possess the athletic ability of the other girls on the team, the father hung up the phone in silence. Why are we afraid of the truth? Our society's veins pulse with relativism. When Jesus dealt with the members of the Sanhedrin two thousand years ago, He experienced their relativism first hand. Jesus called them hypocrites. He tried to make them aware of their false ways. He unleashed His anger in the temple the day He overturned the tables of the sellers and money changers. They made the truth something that was convenient to them. The truth hurts sometimes. It is not always the easiest path to follow. In a culture where we walk the line of political correctness, we avoid the truth because we worry about offending someone.

Many times on my way to school, I would pass a man holding a pro-life sign on the street outside of a local clinic that offered abortion as one of the options to an unplanned pregnancy. This man would carry a sign around his neck for hours each day in all kinds of weather. The signs he carried did not shock you with a graphic photo of an aborted baby, rather his sign usually stated a simple statistic about abortion. He looked emotionless as he held his sign up for the world to see. When I told people about this man, they all seemed to know him. His quiet presence affected so many people. There were others who carried signs outside the clinic, but people seem to notice this particular man. I often wondered, "What kind of person would dedicate so much of their time to the cause of life?" I had to know. So one day I stopped and introduced myself to this man. As I approached him, he seemed a little apprehensive. The clinic made sure that his time outside the clinic would not be pleasant. They would often call the police and accuse him of trespassing. He thought that I had been sent to harass him. He introduced himself as Artie. Artie told me his story. After he had retired, he slipped into a deep depression. He found himself unable to leave his bed. With the help of his wife, Artie looked for a meaningful task that would give him a reason to get out of bed each day. He spoke lovingly about his wife and how she helped lift him out of the depths of his despair. The cause of the unborn had always been close to Artie's heart, so he decided that this would become his new "job."

As Artie and I spoke on this busy thoroughfare, people cursed and screamed insults at him. He didn't flinch when they blasted their horns or yelled at him. Artie explained calmly, "I guess if someone stood outside my house and held up a sign contrary to one of my beliefs, I would be angry too. I just want them to be aware of the truth." So many people conveniently ignore the reality of the unborn. Artie realized that for people to notice him, he would have to move closer to the traffic. Artie is well aware of the relativism of our world. Artie also knows that speaking the truth can be dangerous. He has heard both sides of the debate. Artie knows the truth.

When we watch the news or read the tabloids, we see relativism in motion. Our society has become Godless, because of our fear of offending others. This Godlessness has permeated the morality of our world. In his book *The Philosophy of Jesus*, Peter Kreeft explains:

> And the deepest diagnosis of the root cause of our culture's disease, in a single word, is Christlessness. Worse, it is Christophobia. The strongest answer to moral relativism is not a perfect argument but a perfect person: Christ. For that is concrete evidence, real data, real presence. Meet him, and relativism shrivels like a vampire in the sunlight. The most irrefutable arguments are always facts, data, and concrete reality. For instance, the most effective argument is simply to see one.
>
> That is why the most common operation in America is the only one never seen on any TV or movie screen. The two things that convince people the most are facts and people. Christ is both.

When you live a Christ-centered life, the truth becomes apparent. The murky waters of relativism instantly clear. Following Christ demands making choices. Jesus didn't worry about being politically correct. He looked people directly in the eye and said, "You're wrong," and told them the way things should be. Pope Benedict XVI warns us of the dangers of relativism:

> Having a clear faith, based on the creed of the Church, is often labeled today as fundamentalism, whereas relativism, which is letting oneself be tossed and swept along by every wind of teaching, looks like the only attitude acceptable to today's standards.

Christ calls us to provide balance to the subjective world. The Master brings reality and truth into the chaos of our society. We must become messengers of the truth. The Master exhorts us to bring these truths to others:

1. God exists! Jesus walked this earth to show that God is not a figment of the imagination. We have testimony to His existence from the greatest figures in history. No matter how our society tries to deny His existence, we must not let others push Him aside. We can incorporate God into everything we do. Unveil proof of His existence to others. Do not hesitate to tell His story.

2. We must include God in our lives. There is no substitute for this important relationship. Show others the void that exists in their lives without Him. The Master made Himself present in the lives of the lonely to reveal how we can be transformed with God. Having Christ in our lives gives us meaning and direction. Demonstrate how He helps us to see this world with clarity. Putting our faith and trust in Jesus will bring us fulfillment that we can't find anywhere else.

3. There is no greater symbol of truth than the Cross. The "T" shape of the Cross reminds us of its inevitable Truth. Without the sacrifice of Jesus, we will not be saved. It is through the cross that we see how God loves the world. The Master wants us to embrace the cross and make it our own. Show the truth of the cross to others with a life of faithfulness and prayer. Make the cross more than just an ornament that we display around our necks as jewelry. Present the true cross to others.

4. Christ is truly present in the Eucharist. The Eucharist is not a mere symbol of Jesus. The Master makes this truth perfectly clear. We can truly receive Him and enter into Communion with Jesus in this sacrament. The Eucharist points us to heaven. We take the true presence of Jesus for granted. Make church a priority in your life and bring your family and friends to receive Him.

5. Buying into the values of our culture will bring us sure misery. Our society chooses its doctrines by the way the wind is blowing. Many refuse to believe that the "fetus" inside of a woman is actually a growing child because they want to use abortion as a form of birth control. Many others believe that premarital sex has no consequence on us as human beings because it has become a recreational activity. Others follow the creed of a culture that says that we must look a certain way or own a certain product because this is the only way to find fulfillment. Help others to distinguish between objective and subjective reality. Present the facts and data and show them Jesus. Smash the world of relativism with the hammer of truth.

The Master revealed the truths of the world to His disciples. We must continue to show these truths to those around us. Without the truth of Christ, we will drown in the waters of relativism.

As we navigate though this life, faith in Christ provides our only path to the shore. Without Him as our foundation, we will remain adrift. Allow Jesus to be your beacon in the world of relativism. He will shed light on the things in this life that you can't seem to understand. Find Christ and find the truth.

Keeping the Peace

*First keep the peace within yourself, then
you can also bring peace to others.*

Thomas à Kempis

You can usually tell a Catholic crowd by the way they gravitate to
the back of an auditorium or church. I, too, fall into the category
of the Catholic who rarely sits in the front of their church. As a
new parent, the back of the church became a place that provided
a quick escape if our children were not in the mood to cooperate
at Mass. As we grew accustomed to our usual pew by a particular
stained glass window, our son Alex would ask about the people
in the picture. The story is one familiar to all Christians. When
Mary Magdalene went to the tomb of Jesus to anoint His body,
she realized that He was gone. Distraught, she sat alone and wept.
She had yet to comprehend that Jesus had been raised from the
dead. As Mary cried, the risen Lord came to comfort His friend:

> Jesus said to her, "Woman, why are you weeping? Who
> are you looking for?" She thought it was the gardener

and said to Him, "Sir, if you have carried Him away, tell me where you have laid Him and I will take Him."

When Alex asked, "Who is that and why is she crying?" I had to pause a moment to collect my thoughts. This story was much too complex for a child under the age of two to comprehend. I tried to respond the simplest way possible without losing the meaning of the story. I explained, "That's Jesus and His friend Mary. Jesus is telling her that because He is with her, everything is going to be alright." Even at a young age, I wanted Alex to realize the most important premise of our faith: With Jesus, we can find peace. Peace of heart, peace of mind, and peace of our inner being depend on having Christ in our lives. I wanted Alex to realize that Jesus is the ultimate consoler and peacemaker. As a father, I knew he needed to understand the gift of inner peace that Jesus provides. As John Paul II told us:

> Inner peace comes from knowing that one is loved by
> God and from the desire to respond to His love.

Mary, the mother of Jesus, understood that peace. She would be asked by God to do the unthinkable, sacrifice her child. Yet, she offered no protest or complaint. She willingly submitted to the will of God peacefully. It takes tremendous inner fortitude to face the trials of life as Mary did. Mary lived the Beatitude:

> Blessed are the peacemakers, for they shall be called
> children of God.   (Matthew 5:8)

For the Christian, the goal is to take the peace that Christ provides and bring that peace to others. The pace of our world makes it difficult to find inner consolation. Our tabloid driven society has affected the way in which we relate to each other. We find delight in watching others struggle. Many of our conversations barely rise above a whisper because we are not particularly proud of what we have to say. We spoke about gossip earlier. We can't foster peace when we destroy another with our words. Our neighborhoods become divided because of petty disputes. The people in the office form cliques. Alliances separate, rather than join people. We see conflicts arise every day. Our mission must be to help bring others together. Someone in our office, school, neighborhood, or team needs to say, "Enough!" End the insanity!

There are several things that we can do to resolve conflicts. We must make sure that we practice these in our own lives as well as we try to help others:

1. Teach others to compromise. Meet in the middle. The first rule of relationships is to realize that it is not all about you. Conflicts are rarely resolved if there is no give and take. Ask others to be open-minded of what the other person is thinking.

2. Walk in another's shoes to see how they feel. We have to try to understand what the other person is going through. We have to ask the questions: What made them act that way? Why did they say that? We can never be sure until we look at life from their perspective. Walk in their shoes.

3. Help others to learn that the only way to resolve conflicts is through communication. Without dialogue, a relationship is doomed to failure. Without communication, we cannot know what the other person is thinking. Often, we withdraw and remain silent when we need to talk.

4. Sometimes the best way to end a conflict is by walking away. When confronted by a "no win" situation, it is better to avoid further damaging a relationship by entering into battle. Sometimes one of the parties is not ready to discuss the problem. Cut your losses and leave the debate for another day.

5. A sincere apology can immediately disarm an angry person. Saying, "I'm sorry," can help undo some of the harm caused by the conflict. The admission of guilt is an important step to healing.

6. Lighten the mood. Laughter allows us to forget our problems. It keeps us sane. Humor can help a person see how ridiculous a situation is. I once heard a person say, "He who laughs, lasts." (Mary Poole) Humor will help us to endure the most difficult times.

7. Forgive. Teach others to forgive and to forgive themselves. True peace begins with forgiveness.

In order to be an effective peacemaker, you too must find inner peace. Don't let a frantic world deny you that peace. Slow down the pace to find serenity. Be an instrument of change. Be the voice of reason. Help heal the wounds of conflict. Bridge the gap of a broken relationship. Be the presence of Christ when it seems as if all hope is gone. Calm their hearts and their fears. Remember the only way to be a peacemaker is to be actively participating in the lives of the people around you. Bring His unity to the divided, His humility to the obstinate, and His patience to the weary. Be His peacemaker.

And let the peace of Christ rule in your hearts to which indeed you were called in that one body.
(Colossians 3:15-17)

Love Your Neighbor

Infantile love follows the principle: "I love because I am loved."
Mature love follows the principle: "I am loved because I love."
Immature love says: "I love you because I need you."
Mature love says: "I need you because I love you."

Erich Fromm

Love seems to be the most misused word in the English language today. "I love ice cream," "I love *Seinfeld*," "I love the beach." We tend to throw around a word that has profound meaning. Love is defined as the active care and concern for another. Not only do I desire the well being of another, I am willing to do something about it. The greatest definition of love can be found in the Gospels as the history of salvation unfolds.

Jesus constantly battles the Scribes and the Pharisees during His ministry. Many times they fought over the interpretation of Mosaic Law. Jesus provided insights into Jewish teaching that people had never heard before. During their debates, a discussion over the Ten Commandments arose. When they asked Jesus which of the Ten Commandments held the most importance, He replied:

> Hear O Israel! The Lord our God is Lord alone. You shall love the Lord your God with all your heart, all your soul, with all your mind and all your strength. The second is this: You shall love your neighbor as yourself. There is no other commandment greater than these.
> (Mark 12:29-30)

If you love God and others properly, you will not have any difficulty obeying the commandments. In a selfish world, loving others can be difficult. Jesus realizes the obstacles to love, so He gives us the greatest example of love: Himself. When I was old enough to realize what was happening at church, I remember sitting at Good Friday services and asking, "What's so 'Good' about today?" I saw the way people treated Jesus. I was saddened by the way His best friends betrayed Him. The crowd that had listened to Him preach turned against Him and called for His death. A child, age seven, could not comprehend the "good" qualities of this day whatsoever. But as a Christian explores the Paschal mystery, he sees the beauty of God's love emerge. God gives us Himself as He lays down His life, not only for those who love Him, but for a humanity that has turned its back on Him. Sometimes loving your family and friends can be difficult. How can we, then, love a person who despises us?

Jesus told His followers the parable of the Good Samaritan. The Samaritans were hated by the Jews. They had been brought to Judea after the Assyrians had conquered the Israelites. As foreigners, they were considered outcasts by the Jewish people. In the parable, the only person to stop and help the man who had been beaten by robbers was a Samaritan. Everyone is left asking the question, "Why would a person help someone who despises him?" Jesus challenges us to love everyone, no matter how they treat us.

I spoke about this challenge one day in my senior religion class. One student, Susan, had lost her dad in the World Trade Center on September 11th. As I spoke about how Jesus wanted us to forgive others in every situation, Susan raised her hand. Adamant in her response, Susan pleaded, "I could never love the people who killed my dad!" As her voice cracked, I looked at the sorrow still alive in her teary eyes and I sympathized with her. I told Susan there was no way that most of us could understand the heartache she felt. But as we finished our discussion that day, I asked Susan and the rest of the class to walk in the shoes of Jesus for the last few days of His life. He is betrayed, mocked, tortured and killed. He not only forgave those who sinned against Him, but He freely gave His life so that we may share the gift of eternal life.

On senior retreat, we watch the Czech movie, *Most,* translated *The Bridge*. It is a movie about the loving relationship between a bridge operator and his son. The father and son cherish each moment they spend together. The son sometimes joins the father while he works at the drawbridge. On one fateful day, a train approaches the bridge ahead of schedule. When the son notices the drawbridge in the open position, he tries to assist his father in averting disaster. As he tries to lower the bridge manually, he falls into the gears that operate the bridge. The father must now make a decision: Do I keep the bridge open, kill hundreds of people, but save my son or do I lower the bridge and save a train full of passengers, but sacrifice my son?

During the movie, we get a quick glimpse of the passengers. The self-absorbed, the selfish, the isolated, people immersed in what George Weigel referred to in his book, *Letters to a Young Catholic* as "debonair nihilism." In this type of nihilism, humanity enjoys itself on the way to oblivion. We do not mean to ignore God; we simply replace him with other things. The people on the train represent a society that substitutes God with material possessions.

On the train, a young woman sits alone. Her despair has driven her to leave her family. In her compartment, she prepares heroin that she will inject into her veins. When the train passes the father who has just given his son for the sake of others, her life undergoes conversion. She recognizes what the man has done for her. Her focus shifts from the selfish world in which she lived, to the world of the man who saved her life. At the end of the movie, we see this girl living her new life with a renewed spirit and now with her own child. The child bears a resemblance to the son of the bridge operator. We become images of God as we follow in His ways.

We forsake Him everyday and He still loves us unconditionally. The arms of love never close. His love has no end. God's love, like Himself, is infinite. As we search for the true definition of love, we realize that love helps us to put the emphasis on others. When we make decisions in our lives we should keep the words of St. Augustine in mind, "Love and do whatever you want." When we act with the best interest of others in mind, we are able to make better choices. Love challenges us to get off the couch and help our parents, to leave the warmth of our homes to assist a neighbor in need, to forsake a tight schedule to spend some time in conversation with a lonely soul. Jesus on the cross speaks to us each day and asks, "If I could do this for you, what will you do for others?" As we live out the Christian life, we incorporate the love that flows from God to His creation and give that love to others. In true genuine love, the more we give away the more we receive in return.

Loving other people will fulfill you. Love helps you to find meaning in your life. Give yourself to others. Stop holding back. Love others as the Master loves you. Give His greatest gift to others and change the world with each act of love you perform.

Conversations with God

*The desire is thy prayers; and if thy desire is without ceasing,
thy prayer will also be without ceasing. The continuance
of your longing is the continuance of your prayer.*

Saint Augustine

After His last supper with the apostles, Jesus went to prepare
Himself for His final hours. He took with Him His closest friends:
Peter, James and John. These apostles were with the Lord during the most important moments of His life. They witnessed the
Transfiguration. They saw Lazarus raised from the dead. Now they
were asked by Jesus to accompany Him during His hour of need.
They entered the garden of Gethsemane with Jesus. He instructed
them to remain awake. Jesus knew He wasn't the only one who
needed to spiritually prepare Himself for the next few days. Jesus
recognized the need for prayer. At this moment, it was the most
appropriate thing to do. As He spoke to His Father, He asked for
the strength to complete His mission. Through the power of the
Incarnation, Jesus felt human despair. He experienced the depths
of loneliness and He understood physical suffering. The day had

finally arrived for the plan of salvation to unfold. Jesus needed to feel the presence and consolation of His Father. He shows us that we can conquer all things with God by our side.

Jesus knew the weakness of His friends, so He checked on them to make sure that they were still awake. Even though He desperately desired their companionship, they gave in to their weariness and fell asleep. Jesus reprimanded Peter, James and John, but each time He returned, they were fast asleep. On one side of the garden, we see a man in deep contemplation and prayer and on the other side we find three men who gave in to their weakness and selfishly ignored the wishes of their friend. Putting yourself in God's presence requires us to remove the distractions from our lives.

For me, prayer has always been a challenge. Being plugged into the 24/7 world, I find it hard to separate myself from the shopping list of jobs I have to complete. Even in the quietest of times, my mind zips to another place when I am trying to communicate with God. The way Pope John Paul II prayed always impressed me. He seemed to be transported to another place as he knelt and spoke to God. Amidst the cameras and large crowds he was able to be in solitude with the Father. For me, I try to heed John Paul's advice on prayer.

> Prayer can truly change your life, for it turns your attention away from yourself and directs your mind and heart toward the Lord. If we look only at ourselves, with our limitations and sins, we give way to sadness and discouragement. But if we keep our eyes fixed on the Lord, then our hearts are filled with hope, our minds are washed in the light of truth, and we come to know the fullness of the Gospel with all its promise and life.
> (Meeting with Youth in New Orleans, 1987)

As Jesus spoke to His friends in Gethsemane, He speaks to us today. Prayer keeps us focused. With our eyes and hearts fixed on God, we will remain on the right path, even when our prayers are distracted by the frenzy of our world. The presence of God can ease the craziness of our lives.

Life teaches this important lesson: we must learn to accept the things that we can't understand. Prayer assists us in finding the answers. In the garden, Jesus not only prays for Himself, but He prays for all of humanity. He remembers those who reject God's salvation in His plea to the Father. Jesus shows us that prayer must be unselfish and sincere. Real prayer requires us to put our entire being into it.

Jesus perfects prayer. He presents the pattern for all prayer in the *Our Father*. He shows that the best way to approach God is as a child petitions his "dad." The *Catechism of the Catholic Church* says that this type of prayer implies a close, personal and dependent relationship with God. We hand ourselves over completely to our Father in heaven.

Jesus urges us to pray with the correct intentions. He told His followers the parable of the Pharisee and the Tax Collector. In the story as the Pharisee prays, he focuses on the faults of the tax collector. But in turn when the tax collector prays, he humbly looks to heaven and asks the Lord to forgive him for his errors. We may have the tendency to become self-righteous in our praying. Flannery O'Connor called smugness the great Catholic sin. Jesus wants our hearts in the right place when we pray. It becomes the place to practice our love of God. St. Alphonsus Liguori said, "Prayer is the blessed furnace in which the holy fire of love is kindled and kept alive." This fire must be tended daily to keep it burning strong. Communication improves every relationship.

We find it difficult to separate ourselves from our computers and our cell phones. We feel out of touch when we shut them off when we sit in the movies or go to church. We should have the same approach when it comes to our relationship with God. How long has it been since you have had a good heart to heart talk with the Lord? What keeps you from conversing with Him on a regular basis? Open up the lines of communication. Make an effort to speak to Him every day. Thank Him for the gifts in your life. Take a moment during a busy day to acknowledge His presence. Seek His advice and consolation. Look at the way the Master prayed. Put your heart and soul into every word. Share your most difficult times and your moments of joy with God. He longs to hear your voice.

Stop making excuses. Talk to Him!

The Humble One

*We serve God by serving others. The world defines
greatness in terms of power, possessions, prestige, and
position. If you can demand service from others, you've arrived.
In our self-serving culture with its "me-first" mentality,
acting like a servant is not a popular concept.*

Rick Warren

Before Jesus celebrated His last Passover with His disciples, He
took off His outer garments and prepared to wash the feet of His
friends. Jesus used moments like this to teach. He wanted to stress
that His death would cleanse humanity of its sin. Jesus also needed
to show the apostles a model of service that would be necessary
if they would successfully carry out the mission of the Church.
This extraordinary act served as a symbol of service, humility and
purification. We commemorate this event in a special way at our
Holy Thursday liturgy. Jesus exalts His apostles and reminds them
of the importance of being humble at the same time. Simon Peter
resisted Jesus at first, but the Master reprimanded him. Unless he
allowed Jesus to wash him, Peter would not share in His kingdom.
After finishing the washing, Jesus explained His actions:

Do you realize what I have done for you? You call me Teacher and Master, for indeed, I am. If I therefore, the Master has washed your feet, you ought to wash one another's feet. I have given you a model to follow so that as I have done for you, you should also do. Amen, amen I say to you, no slave is greater than his master, nor any messenger greater than the one who sent him.   (John 13:13-16)

As children, we played the game King of the Hill. We raced to become the person who dominated the top spot. We scratched our way to the top of the hill. We spend our lives climbing the ladder of success. Many times we push aside others who stand in our way. Many people profess their devotion to what we call the un-Holy Trinity: me, myself and I. Being a singer-songwriter, musician, choir director, and teacher, I witness people promoting themselves daily. They plead, "I should have the lead in the play," "That promotion belongs to me," or "My voice is better than his!" People fail to see the importance of humility. Many build themselves up by tearing others down. They could learn from the way Jesus lived His Life. We sacrifice anything to achieve our goals. Jesus reminded us that along our journey, we must be willing to serve others. Our success will be measured by what we can sacrifice for others in need. Jesus recognized the competitive spirit within us. He dealt with the pride and rivalry of His own disciples. James and John fought openly about their place in the kingdom of heaven. Jesus reminded all of the apostles of the paradox they faced as leaders of the Church:

Whoever wishes to be great among you will be your servant; whoever wishes to be the first among you will be servant of all. For the Son of Man did not come to

be served, but to serve and to give His life as a ransom
for many.   (Mark 10:43-45)

Jesus demands that same response from us. The more we
acquire, the more we should give away. Many of us forget about
this as we aim to succeed at any cost. How many of us consciously
serve others?

Recently, a former student requested that my choir sing at
her mother's funeral. Many important people attended the funeral
including our Bishop, William Murphy. I was impressed by the
way that the Bishop and others spoke about Peg. Peg lived her life
with simplicity and grace. She exhibited class without putting on
airs as many people of affluence do. Peg and her husband Lewis
were blessed with a life of comfort. Lewis, a successful business
man, served on several executive boards. His business savvy and
hard work brought his family a life of luxury.

Even though her formal name was Margaret, she always
introduced herself simply as "Peg." When Peg arrived at any
event, she always asked, "What can I do to help?" Her willingness to serve made her stand out in a crowd. Peg's generous spirit
quietly spread throughout her parish and diocese. Her passion for
Catholic education fostered an organization called "Tomorrow's
Hope." Peg anonymously assisted those who could not afford to
send their children to parochial school. She turned her garage into
a workstation to assemble care packages for soldiers fighting in
Iraq. She had lived through the Vietnam War and Peg wanted to
make sure that these soldiers were not forgotten.

Peg worked diligently to support Regina Residence and
Bethany House. These homes provided an environment for unwed mothers. Their goal was to assist these mothers get on their
feet after giving birth to their babies. Peg also loved the arts. Her

work with Career Transitions for Dancers helped those who had grown too old to continue dancing, to find other jobs. Peg would be the first one with a broom in her hands at her daughter's dance recitals.

When Peg was asked by Bishop Murphy to serve on the Board of Catholic Charities, she reminded him that having cancer might prevent her from fulfilling her duties. At the funeral, Bishop Murphy stated that although Peg was never able to attend any board meetings, no one had ever contributed to Catholic Charities as Peg had done. Living a life of service made Peg who she was, a true disciple of Christ. Everything she touched was touched with the grace and love of Christ. As Christ had served humanity, so did she.

God had blessed Peg and Lewis with many wonderful gifts. By living out the message in the Parable of the Talents, they made sure to share their gifts with others. Even though they were in a position to be served, they chose to serve others instead. Our lives are transformed as we transform the lives of others. Working behind the scenes does not usually gain us recognition. It might not win us any awards. It does, however, put us next to Christ in His willingness to serve others. The King of Priests urges us to minister to others. Use your God-given gifts to build up others and the community around you. Stand from the table and bow before others. Serving others will gain you a better seat at His table in heaven. As He told His disciples, real joy will not be found in the power, prestige or status of this world. He points us to our place in His kingdom. Serve others and reserve your place.

Caught, Not Taught

One looks back with appreciation to the brilliant teachers, but with gratitude to those who touched our human feelings. The curriculum is so much necessary raw material, but warmth is the vital element for the growing plant and for the soul of the child.

Carl Jung

We can all remember one particular teacher who affected us in a special way. We may not be able to recall the chapter of the book they taught that had an impact on us, but we do remember what they said and how they said it. Their words remain with us to this very day. As a teacher, there is no greater gift than the student who returns to the campus and seeks you out. He or she yearns to tell you about a life lesson that was revealed in your class. Your words have had an impact, even years after the final bell rang and the class had ended. These moments make a teacher realize their true vocation as a teacher.

There are many references to Jesus as a "teacher." His disciples called Him "Rabbi." People questioned Him on His knowledge of the Jewish faith, the Scriptures, and Mosaic Law. They asked Him questions about this life and the next. He was the ultimate teacher. Attendance in His class was not mandatory; however, a passing grade meant eternal life in His kingdom. His lesson started with the theme of love, and ended with love. He dealt with everything else in between. Jesus taught life lessons. He gave His students a guide to daily living and if they followed His plan, they could find real happiness. He awakened their hearts and minds. Nothing could hinder this happiness if they remembered what He taught them. He would open a door that no one could close. Jesus was the consummate teacher, the kind of teacher everyone looks up to. They couldn't wait for His class to begin. In comparison, everything else seemed trivial.

Our lives begin with our most influential educators, our parents. They teach us to talk, to walk, to behave a certain way. In short, they give us the basic tools that we need to live. Teachable moments occur every day. Our parents define who we are. They show us that our greatest lessons occur outside the classroom. No matter what we choose as our career, we all become teachers at one time or another. There are people around us who look for our wisdom. Christ the teacher invites us to peek into His lesson plans. He encourages us to join the noblest profession. The temple in Jerusalem, the Mount of the Beatitudes, the home of Martha and Mary all became His classroom. As we look to the Teaching Christ, we can apply His lessons to everyday living.

Jesus made His message real and understandable. He spoke to the most educated members of the Jewish faith as well as to illiterate commoners. His parables were meant to entice the listener to ask questions. Education begins with curiosity. He wanted His disciples to comprehend the kingdom of God. Parables conveyed this enigmatic truth in an understandable way. But even with His clever teaching techniques, Jesus would never have been an effective teacher if He did not possess the essential qualities of a caring educator. Jesus exhibits tremendous patience throughout His entire ministry. He gently corrects the apostles in their moments of ignorance. He enlightens His reluctant student Nicodemus and helps him to understand the notion of being "born again." He saw the clueless looks of His followers and never despaired. A teacher can feel very much alone in front of the classroom, asking, "Am I actually inspiring my students?" Jesus probably felt that same frustration as He preached. Look to Jesus to find the strength and courage to teach. His example can be used in every situation. Relate a past experience to others. Help them learn from your mistakes and give them hope when you share triumphs. Simplify a complex situation with calming words of reassurance. Diffuse worry with your tranquil presence. Inspire others to grow through education.

The compassion of Jesus filled the void in the hearts of His followers. They came to Him seeking anything He would be willing to give. Their emptiness seems to fade when they listened to Him speak. He could have spoken about compassion, but without His living example, His message would have seemed meaningless. He listened to their problems and offered His advice. Many of our conversations begin with the words, "How are you?", but we do not expect to have to listen to their problems if they decide to share them with us. Jesus encourages us to have true communication with those around us. Lend a compassionate ear and offer a kind word of advice to those who seek our help.

Jesus displayed the greatest characteristic of teaching through His dedication and selflessness. Always willing to give His all, His greatest lesson is taught on Good Friday. He leaves His students a message and blueprint for life. In order to love, we must do anything for those around us. The greatest lesson took a lifetime to prepare, but the effects of His lesson are eternal. In order to illustrate His teaching, He paid the ultimate price. He knew that in order to mold us His message would have to be radical. As Helen Keller said:

> Character cannot be developed in ease and quiet. Only through experience of trial and suffering can the soul be strengthened, ambition inspired, and success achieved.

His students would never forget this incredible class. He showed His followers that by putting our trust in Him, He would never let us down.

At Kellenberg Memorial High School where I teach, we use a philosophy cultivated by our president, Father Philip Eichner. He says that education is "caught, not taught." By immersing a student into an atmosphere of faith, he or she can be transformed. As we mentioned before, some of the most effective lessons take place outside of the classroom. When the Marianist brothers took over Kellenberg, they began building courtyards and fish ponds with the idea of creating an atmosphere of civility, order and respect. Some who were not confident that the students would accept these nice changes warned Father Philip that the framed artwork that he placed throughout the school would be destroyed by the students. He would not relent, insisting that students would appreciate the beauty of their school. His school would not only educate the minds of the students, but their hearts as well. The pictures were only part of his "atmosphere of faith." He commissioned artwork that adorned the chapels and hallways. He landscaped the grounds of the campus to include koi ponds and lush courtyards. Peacocks even roamed the grounds. He made the high school a beautiful place to grow for the young Christian adult and the teacher as well.

Those who followed Jesus felt different in His presence. His atmosphere of faith was created with His words and reached its culmination with His death and resurrection. You need only to gaze upon a cross to see His message. He wants us to join Him as He teaches His curriculum. Point others to God. Teach them about a moral life. Class never ends for Jesus. His most fulfilling lesson is waiting to be taught. Change lives as He did. Joining Him in this mission may have its cost. Some will be disinterested, some may even be angry. But for those who understand His message, they will be changed forever. Become a teacher like Jesus. It is a job with the greatest benefits. Create your own atmosphere of faith and watch their eyes open when they discover the point of your class.

LESSON

Lean on Me

*The whole Christian life is a life in which the further a
person progresses, the more he has to depend directly
on God.... The more we progress, the less we are self-sufficient.
The more we progress, the poorer we get so that the man who has
progressed most, is totally poor – he has to depend directly
on God. He's got nothing left in himself.*

Thomas Merton

A few years ago, we had the opportunity to refine our twelfth grade religion curriculum. After the dust had settled, we agreed that the core of the course on apologetics would revolve around Father William O'Malley's *Meeting The Living God*, George Weigel's *Letters To A Young Catholic*, Mitch Albom's *Tuesdays With Morrie* and Christopher West's *The Good News About Love, Sex, and Marriage*. These books carried the message that we wanted to convey to our students. Father O'Malley's thesis on God's existence is masterful. Christopher West has made his personal mission to teach Pope John Paul II's Theology of the Body. Papal biographer, George Weigel is one of the greatest Catholic voices of our generation and Mitch Albom's popular existential book has become a modern classic.

After a full academic year of study, the seniors prepare for their comprehensive exams. Inevitably, I tell my students this: "In the years to come, you may not remember a quotation we discussed or even what our textbooks were about. I want you remember one thing: You must include a relationship with God in your lives." We all need to understand that life without Jesus Christ is one without true joy and fulfillment. I look in their eyes to see if they truly comprehend the meaning of these words. Thankfully after a year of saying this hundreds of times, most of the students do understand it. As Jesus told us when He described Himself as the Vine, without Him we can do nothing. I occasionally begin my class with this verse from the book of the prophet Isaiah to describe the awesomeness of God:

> Do you not know or have you not heard? The LORD is the eternal God, Creator of the ends of the earth. He does not faint nor grow weary, and His knowledge is beyond scrutiny. He gives strength to the fainting; for the weak He makes vigor abound. Though young men faint and grow weary, and youths stagger and fall, Those who hope in the LORD will renew their strength, they will soar as with eagles' wings; They will run and not grow weary, walk and not grow faint.
> (Isaiah 40:28-31)

The students seem amazed when they find out I sold my business to come to teach. "Was the business making money when you sold it?" they ask. "Of course it was," I answer. "Then why would you sell it?" they argue. It's the same conversation every year. They can't seem to understand that a person would choose a lifestyle where you could spend more time with your family even if that meant forsaking a larger salary. I explain to them that my delicatessen yielded many fruitful years. I drove the best foreign cars and had the opportunity to travel around the world. But I realized that money did not make me happy. In fact, I came to realize that nothing made sense without God.

People at the time of Jesus worried about the same things we do. Jesus warned His followers about depending on material things rather than God:

> Why are you anxious about clothes? Learn from the way the wild flowers grow. They do not work or spin. But I tell you that not even Solomon in all his splendor was clothed like one of them. If God so clothes the grass of the field, which grows today and is thrown into the oven tomorrow, will He not much more provide for you, O you of little faith? So do not worry and say, "What are we to eat?" or "What are we to drink?" or "What are we to wear?" All these things the pagans seek. Your heavenly Father knows that you need them all. But seek first the kingdom of God and His righteousness, and all these things will be given you besides. Do not worry about tomorrow; tomorrow will take care of itself. Sufficient for a day is its own evil.
> (Matthew 6:28-34)

So many people depend on the wrong things for true happiness. We spoke about our reliance on material possessions earlier. We fail to surrender to the One who knows everything and is everything. I grew up in a house where theology was simple: depend on God and things will work out. My parents saw their siblings die much too young. They buried a niece who died at the age of twelve from cancer. Their creed never changed: "Put your trust in God." Their words of wisdom would remain constant. They seemed to be at peace with life even in the most turbulent of times. Suffering can rattle our faith and trust in God. My parents taught me that during these times we must lean on Him more than ever:

> Blessed is the man who trusts in the LORD, whose hope is the LORD. He is like a tree planted beside the waters that stretches out its roots to the stream: It fears not the heat when it comes, its leaves stay green; In the year of drought it shows no distress, but still bears fruit. (Jeremiah 17:7-8)

As Jesus preached the coming of the kingdom of God, He urged people to include God in their lives. He preached that a relationship with God will give us security and bring us everlasting joy. Jesus, however, did not mean the type of dependence where we *only* call upon Him when we are in trouble. So many people only turn to God in moments of crisis. Dependence on God requires us to hold up our end of the covenant. Faithfulness, love and devotion must be part of this covenant. In the pivotal moments in the life of Jesus, He shows us the total and complete trust that He has for the Father. In these instances, He demonstrates His dependence through prayer. Let your lives be open to the presence of God. Let Him work within every aspect of your being. Allow Him to be your compass in the darkness. Seek His warmth in the bitter cold. Rest your weary head upon His shoulder. He will be your strength when you can't continue. He wants you to lean upon Him.

St. Teresa of Avila wrote this beautiful meditation on her willingness to surrender to the Lord:

> Let nothing affright thee,
> Nothing dismay thee,
> All is passing,
> God ever remains.
> Patience obtains all
> Whoever possesses God
> Cannot lack anything
> God alone suffices.

LESSON

My Best Friend

*When we honestly ask ourselves which person in our lives
means the most to us, we often find that it is those who,
instead of giving much advice, solutions, or cures, have chosen
rather to share our pain and touch our wounds with a gentle
and tender hand. The friend who can be silent with us in a moment
of despair or confusion, who can stay with us in an hour
of grief and bereavement, who can tolerate not knowing,
not curing, not healing and face with us the reality of our
powerlessness, that is a friend who cares.*

Henri Nouwen

When I was in the third grade, the students in my class would take
turns reading aloud E.B. White's classic, *Charlotte's Web*. On the
Arable farm, a group of pigs are born. When the daughter, Fern,
finds out that her father has gone to the barn to kill the runt of the
litter, she intervenes and convinces him to temporarily spare his
life. Wilbur, as she calls him, is sent to the farm of Fern's uncle.
However, a pig's life expectancy is limited due to the nature of
a livestock farm and, unless something unusual occurs, Wilbur
will become someone's dinner. Wilbur tries to adjust to life in his

new home. A spider named Charlotte responds to Wilbur's need for a friend. She dedicates herself to saving his life through the ingenious ploy of spinning words in her web.

As the story unfolds, the messages of Charlotte's webs bring Wilbur notoriety. He becomes a celebrity of sorts and thus his life is spared. Charlotte describes her act of friendship as a means of elevating her otherwise ordinary life:

> We're born, we live a little while, we die. A spider's life can't help being something of a mess, with all this trapping and eating flies. By helping you, perhaps I was trying to lift up my life a trifle. Heaven knows anyone's life can stand a little of that.   (*Charlotte's Web*)

Charlotte shows Wilbur and the rest of the animals in the barn the meaning of friendship. This classic has taught so many young people the meaning of friendship. Friendships change us. Our friendships are different than our other relationships. We choose our friends. We bond with friends because we have things in common. We like the same sports or the same music. We can talk about our common interests for hours. We laugh at inside jokes that others may not find funny. We love the time we spend together and miss each other when we are apart.

Jesus surrounded Himself with His closest friends. We see in the Gospels that the friends of Jesus do not necessarily always understand Him. Even worse, they are not always loyal to Him. Jesus was honest about how He felt about failed personal commitments. The Master let them know that their temporary failures did not affect His acceptance of them. Even their failure to remain loyal to Him did not lead Him to reject them. His friendship is unconditional. He does want His disciples to be responsible for their actions, however. When Jesus returns to visit His friends after the resurrection, He approaches Peter who had denied Him three times the night before He was put to death. Jesus asks Peter, "Simon, son of John do you love me more than these?" Peter responded, "Of course, Lord; you know that I love you!" But Jesus asks Peter the question two more times. He will not let Peter off the hook without his learning a lesson from his mistake. Jesus wants him to understand the importance of love in their friendship. Jesus needs Peter to incorporate the love he has for Jesus into his love for the Church. The new leader of the Church must change before taking the reins from Jesus. Peter must shepherd his flock with that love. The Master shows His apostles that love and discipleship begin with friendship. Jesus forms a relationship with us that will continue forever.

Jesus became close friends with Martha, Mary and Lazarus. When Jesus heard the news that Lazarus had died, He said:

> Our friend Lazarus has fallen asleep; but I go, that I may awaken him out of sleep.　　　　(John 11:11)

When the sisters of Lazarus greeted Jesus as He entered Bethany, they showed their trust and faith in Him. Even though Jesus had the power to restore the life of Lazarus, He wept as He approached the tomb of His friend. It saddened Jesus to see His friend suffer and his sisters mourn the loss of their brother.

Jesus offered a unique type of friendship where self-interest, self-preoccupation and selfishness no longer took center stage. Rather, the Master's friendships possessed the qualities of self-sacrifice and self-surrender. Jesus does not abandon His friends when they abandon Him. His friendship lasts for an eternity. He will not forsake us when we make a mistake. A deep and personal relationship with Christ keeps us focused on the needs of others. This must become a priority in every friendship we have. Whether we stand in joy with another as at Cana or in sorrow at the foot of the cross, we learn what it is to be a true friend with Jesus.

In our "disposable" society where we are used to throwing things away when they are no longer useful, we tend to have very little patience in our relationships. Small disagreements shatter our friendships. The Master demonstrated the commitment, forgiveness and trust needed in every friendship. Jesus took the bond of friendship to a whole new level. Denial and betrayal did not prevent Jesus from remaining friends with those who failed Him. The friendship of Christ is steadfast. Jesus wanted His friends to learn from their mistakes. Through His friendship, Jesus tried to elevate His disciples. I always ask my students, "Do your friends make you a better person or do they drag you down?" and in turn, "What kind of example do you give your friends?" Jesus showed His friends the beauty of true friendship by how He lived. Through every word and deed, Jesus displayed how a friend should act. Jesus demonstrated that true friendship does not allow jealousy and envy to get in the way. We must be able to share these qualities in our relationships as well. Following the example of Jesus, we can lead our friends to living more fruitful lives.

The Master knows everything about us and yet He still loves us for who we are. The Master has called us each by name to enter into friendship with Him. A good friend has the ability to gently tell us when we have gone astray. The Master wants to be honest with us and share this honesty with others. Good friends have the ability to look each other in the eyes and speak the truth.

Exhibit the friendship of Christ in all of your relationships. Be there for your friends. When our friends are weary and feel as if they can't continue, we must carry them as He carries us.

His strength can help us through any situation. Our fortitude can bear the burden for others. Our friends need to know how we feel about them. This love should be evident in our faithfulness and trust. The companionship of Jesus never leaves us alone. Our earthly friendships must be an extension of our relationship with Jesus. Your presence in a time of sadness or gentle words in a difficult moment can make a tremendous difference. Even standing in silence with a friend can help them through the darkest of times. Extend the hands of love, as Christ extends His arms in friendship to all of humanity. Show your friends the love of the Master in all you do.

> My command is this: Love each other as I have loved you. Greater love has no one than this, that he lay down his life for his friends. You are my friends if you do what I command. I no longer call you servants, because a servant does not know his master's business. Instead, I have called you friends, for everything that I learned from my Father I have made known to you.
> (John 15:12)

Bread from Heaven

*Our own belief is that the renovation of the world will be
brought about only by the Holy Eucharist.*

Pope Leo XIII

As a teacher of seniors in high school, you see the seeds of apathy begin to take root in October. By March, senioritis is in full bloom. The students snicker when you assign homework. They roll their eyes when you demand their attention. Our seniors visit Disney World a few weeks before they take their final exams. After they arrive home from the trip, getting them to do any work is like drawing blood from a stone. Many Catholics suffer from the epidemic of apathy. They find many reasons to avoid weekly Mass. The pressures of a busy world exhaust us. God is not a priority. We pile on the excuses of how Mass bores us or how we feel disconnected from the Church, rather than make an effort to spend an hour in worship on Sunday. Catholics of every age find reasons to do something else. Unfortunately, by missing Mass, we lose out on the greatest gift that Jesus gave us—His Body and Blood.

Throughout this book, we talk about what we can learn from Jesus. In the Eucharist, we have the ability to become one with Jesus. The Eucharist fulfills Christ's promise of His presence in our midst. Through this Sacrament we encounter His endless love. We are invited to the altar that commemorates the sacrifice of the Lamb, given to us to save us from our sins. But there are so many of us who refuse His invitation. As St. Angela of Foligno said:

> If we but paused for a moment to consider attentively what takes place in this Sacrament, I am sure that the thought of Christ's love for us would transform the coldness of our hearts into a fire of love and gratitude.

The Eucharist compensates for the selfishness within our hearts and calls us to love others as Jesus loves us. In Holy Communion, we receive the gift of His humanity as we share in His gift of redemption. We are united with Christ on His cross and given the opportunity to experience His profound sacrifice. St. Francis de Sales points us to Christ in this meditation:

> When you have received Him, stir up your heart to do Him homage; speak to Him about your spiritual life, gazing upon Him in your soul where He is present for your happiness; welcome Him as warmly as possible, and behave outwardly in such a way that your actions may give proof to all of His Presence.

A few years ago, a book called *The Secret* was on the best seller list. The book stated that positive thinking would help us do amazing things and attain anything we truly desired. This self-help guide failed to mention the real secret to happiness: Communion with Jesus Christ. The book mistakenly teaches that our desire for happiness would be fulfilled if we believe in ourselves. But our existence without true communion with Jesus will leave us empty and alone. He wants to transform us. This process begins with our reception of the Eucharist. Holy Communion allows Him to work in us in a special way so that we may go out and share Him with the rest of the world. The command, "Do this in memory of me," reminds us to make Christ a priority in our lives. His presence fills the emptiness in our hearts and allows us to join Him. We will never achieve this communion if we remain isolated and refuse to receive Him. St. Augustine reminds us of the importance of recognizing the true presence of Jesus in our lives:

> Recognize in this bread what hung on the cross, and in this chalice what flowed from His side... whatever was in many and varied ways announced beforehand in the sacrifices of the Old Testament pertains to this one sacrifice which is revealed in the New Testament.
> (From the writings of St. Augustine,
> Sermon 3, 2; circa A.D. 410)

On senior retreat, our students spend an hour in Eucharistic Adoration. They always comment on how this is their favorite part of the two day retreat. For many students, this can be a very emotional experience. They realized that something has been missing without Christ in their lives. They have filled their lives with empty distractions that have kept them away from true communion with God. They feel spiritually reconnected through their time with Jesus. After Adoration, the students have an opportunity to receive the Sacrament of Reconciliation. Amazingly, most of the students go to Confession, even those who have not received the sacrament since they went for the first time as second graders. Spending time with Jesus can lead us to incredible possibilities. We often forget that Jesus has made Himself so accessible to us.

We spend our lives constantly running around without time to sit and put ourselves in the presence of God. Eucharistic Adoration allows us to do just that.

If you have not spent time with Jesus in Eucharistic Adoration, I highly recommend that you try it. It has worked wonders for me. In quiet contemplation, I have been able to bring my deepest cares and concerns to Jesus. I feel different after spending time face to face with Him. Pope John Paul II urged Catholics to spend time with Jesus in Adoration:

> The Church and the world have great need of Eucharistic adoration. Jesus waits for us in this Sacrament of love. Let us be generous with our time in going to meet Him in adoration and contemplation full of Faith. And let us be ready to make reparation for the great faults and crimes of the world. May our adoration never cease.
> (*Dominicae Cenae*: Letter to Priests,
> Holy Thursday, 1980)

As we approach the time to receive Jesus in the Holy Sacrament of the Eucharist, we utter the words that "we are not worthy to receive Him." Jesus makes our communion with Him possible through the grace and redemption of His sacrifice on the cross. Through His incarnation Jesus became part of humanity, through Holy Communion we enter into the glory of His heavenly realm. Don't deprive yourself of His greatest gift. He awaits you each day at Mass. His invitation to "take and eat" always stands. Make time to visit Him and you will see the difference in your life. The banquet has been prepared at great cost, but the only thing required of you will be your time and desire to change. Change and allow Him to be part of you. Become part of Christ and let Him transform you.

Measure Twice, Cut Once

*By a Carpenter mankind was made,
and only by that Carpenter can mankind be remade.*

Desiderius Erasmus

A simple object like wood held such tremendous significance in the Scriptures. Jesus, born in a stable, was placed by His mother in a wooden feeding trough. The manger became one of the greatest symbols of humility. During the "hidden years" of Jesus, our Savior worked with wood each day in a carpenter's shop with His earthly foster father. When the Romans executed Jesus, they nailed His body to a cross. The cross has endured as the representation of love and grace.

In his book, *God Came Near*, Max Lucado offers a fascinating meditation on when Jesus worked as a carpenter before He began His ministry. As He cleaned up at the end of a long day, Jesus swept the floor. His eyes can't help but notice the nails in the pile of sawdust. Being all-knowing, Jesus thought about the day of His crucifixion where nails will hold His body to a cross. He contemplated the agony of His sacrifice for humanity. The day will soon arrive when Jesus must leave the safety of the carpentry shop and enter a world of rejection and despair. What skills from His time as a carpenter will He bring with Him as He starts His mission? What lessons can Jesus the carpenter teach us as we live out our own earthly mission?

It should not be a surprise to us that Jesus held an occupation where He created something new every day. After all, He was the Creator of all things. A carpenter takes time to stand back and admire his masterpiece. As He did with His heavenly Father, I am sure that He and Joseph gazed upon their creations with pride. Jesus inspires us to share in His creation and to be proud of our own creations. As parents, He calls upon us to bring new life into the world. He encourages all people to protect His most precious creation in every way possible. The protection of the unborn and the care of the elderly are issues to which we are especially called to respond. We can never ignore the dignity of human life.

A carpenter must be able to see the whole picture. Every cut of wood will affect the final product. If one step is missed or one mistake is made, it changes the end result. Jesus urged us to fix mistakes as they happen. We think that if we bury a mistake, it will go away. Unfortunately, many times, things only become worse. I have seen many students who have missed a deadline on a project neglect to mention anything because they feel that it will only draw attention to their error. Admit when things go askew. Take the time to correct things before they get out of hand. Things will fall into place if we take the time to repair our missteps when they occur. Jesus also wanted us to examine our role in this world and how our actions affect those around us.

We should never minimize the importance of everything we do. Jesus, the carpenter, reminded us that every action is of consequence. The things we do may have a ripple effect in the world in which we live. A thoughtful word may lead to another. An act of forgiveness may lead another to forgive. He urged us to be actors and not reactors. We must determine our actions and not allow ourselves to fall victim to what others say and do. We must initiate goodwill and love in society.

His time in the wood shop showed Jesus the importance of planning. But no matter how well thought out our plan might be, Jesus knew that things can and do go wrong. We need to expect the unexpected. Jesus reminds us to face life's challenges head on. When adversity presents itself, the way we handle it will determine whether or not we will be happy in this life. Concentration camp survivor and psychologist Victor Frankl said, "Everything can be taken from a man except... the last of the human freedoms — to choose one's attitude in any given set of circumstances, to choose one's own way." We do not determine what happens in life, but we do decide how we react to what occurs in our lives. I have witnessed too many people who planned every aspect of their lives only to have their plans shattered by an unexpected tragedy. We need to emulate Jesus in His hours of despair. Even on Good Friday, we see Jesus acting with love.

As Jesus worked, the nature of manual labor caused Him to have many blisters. All carpenters encounter nicks and bruises, no matter how skilled they may be. Physical labor takes its toll on the body. No matter how achy he may feel, the carpenter continues to work. The project will not be completed if the carpenter focuses on his pain. Jesus pushes us to work through our pain and disappointment. Life sometimes leaves us beaten and bruised, but we must learn from the carpenter to go on no matter what the circumstance may be. His days as a carpenter prepared Jesus for the journey to Calvary. Jesus showed tremendous strength and courage as He endured a brutal beating on

Good Friday. His ability to complete His mission with love and dignity gives us a beautiful example of perseverance. The next time we feel that we can't go on, we need to look to Jesus for the bravery to continue.

You would not encounter too many carpenters who were impulsive as they practiced their craft. A carpenter must exhibit patience during every step of the project. The best craftsmen take time as they plan their next move. During His ministry, Jesus faced skeptics trying to trick Him, the uneducated who failed to understand His message, and ignorant disciples who subjectively put their own spin on His teachings. Jesus patiently dealt with those who deserved kind and gentle guidance. Practicing patience can bring us peace of heart and mind in our lives. We encounter difficult people and situations every day: parents who do not understand us; students who refuse to focus in class; a slow driver in front of us; a neighbor who thinks that you have nothing to do but talk to them. Stepping back will help us to think about the way we want to proceed. Leonardo DaVinci said this about patience:

> Patience serves as a protection against wrongs as clothes do against cold. For if you put on more clothes as the cold increases, it will have no power to hurt you. So in like manner you must grow in patience when you meet with great wrongs, and they will then be powerless to vex your mind.

Ask Him for patience, He will help you through the most difficult of situations.

Jesus the carpenter shows us how to solve the problems we face. Somehow, the pieces will all come together. We can endure all things, if we keep Him in our heart. A life with Christ provides the same balance that a carpenter demonstrates in his work. One move must counter the next: An act of love to the moment of hurt; a word of respect to the words of disdain; a kind smile to the heartache of loss. Be the strength of the carpenter to others. Set His example in the town where you live. Allow the carpenter's words, "measure twice, cut once," be the mantra that helps you in your relationships. Our relationships are our most important possessions. We need to use the care of the carpenter to sculpt these relationships. Treat these relationships like a master carpenter handles his work of art. Stand back and find solutions to your problems. Demonstrate patience as you build a life constructed with the love of the Master carpenter Himself. Let us be creators as Christ has created. The more time we put into our creation, the better it will be. Place yourself in the carpenter's shop in Nazareth. Enjoy the simplicity of His life and make it your own. Learn from the Master how to make something beautiful out of this life.

The Big Payoff

Heaven wheels above you, displaying
to you her eternal glories, and still your eyes
are on the ground.

Dante Alighieri

Talk to any Christian about the topic of heaven and you will have a fascinating discussion. Christians are obsessed with eternal life. And why not? Joking aside, the possibilities are endless. In my classes, my students ask a multitude of questions on the subject. The apostles questioned Jesus about heaven. They wanted to know about their final reward. They thought that since they knew the CEO, they would be given special privileges in His kingdom. We want to know about our final reward. We go to Church, we try to live a good, moral life and we ask for forgiveness when we sin — all because we desire entrance into His heavenly realm. Everything in the life of the Christian seems to affect whether or not we deserve our place in heaven.

Jesus spoke often about heaven: He told His followers that they must embrace God's kingdom. The ageless fascination with the notion of heaven revolves around our mortality. We know that no one avoids death. The older we get, the faster the years seem to fly by. When we look at our earthly existence and compare it to the age of the universe in which we live, we realize that our lives last only a blink of an eye. Blaise Pascal's famous thesis, called *The Wager,* urges people to bet on God's existence because our reward is the possibility of eternal life.

Our human inclination pushes us to find out about the unknown. In our society, there is a great interest in mediums, people who claim that they can speak to the deceased. Several shows on television feature mediums and their "conversations" with the dead. A few people I know have sought the assistance of mediums in trying to contact their deceased spouses. I do not believe in mediums, but I do understand their interest in finding out whether or not their lost beloved has found eternal happiness. Selfishly, it would be nice to have an advanced scouting report on what heaven is like.

Jesus sheds light on the mysterious kingdom of heaven in the Gospels. We learn the following:

1. *The way to heaven is through a relationship with Jesus Christ.* The Master refers to Himself as the "gate for the sheep" (John 10:8). For us to enter the sheepfold (the kingdom of heaven) we must enter through Jesus Christ. Living a life patterned after the Shepherd will bring us eternity with Him. It is through Jesus and in Jesus we find salvation and grace. Follow His path and find heaven. He opens the door and leads us to happiness. Share in His gift of the kingdom.

2. *Earthly treasure is temporary and will mean nothing in the kingdom of heaven.* Jesus said that material goods are subject to "moth, decay and thieves." When we place our emphasis on temporal goods, we miss out on building up heavenly treasure. Like the farmer who built another barn to hold his surplus of grain, we will lose all of our material possessions when God calls us home to heaven. The love of objects leaves us wanting more. The love of God and others will bring us infinite joy.

3. *Heaven begins now.* Our eternal relationship depends on how we relate to God on earth. If we define heaven as our eternal union with God, we must begin our communion with Him now. A heavenly relationship with God can't begin with the flip of a switch when we die. We must nurture this relationship. Don't wait until it's too late. Talk to Him. Pray at every opportunity. Ask Him for the courage to live a moral life. Visit Him as often as you can. Receive Him in the Eucharist. Remember the words of Jesus, "The kingdom of God is at hand." Live as if He stands next to you, because He does. Find the joy of heaven in every day that you live. Being with God will bring you a happiness that will prepare you for life everlasting.

4. *We must spread the word of His kingdom without fear.* As Jesus told us in Matthew 10:26: "There are people who will renounce any thought of God's presence among us." People refuse to accept God into their lives and are threatened by our faith. Jesus warns us that there is a great chasm between those who accept His kingdom and those who no not. The words of Jesus were reiterated by Pope John Paul II on many occasions, "Be not afraid." Your faith will bring you eternal rewards.

The message of the Master is clear in His ministry: We must enter the kingdom when we are called. His calling begins in this life. Embrace the way of life that will lead you into eternity. Incorporate God into every aspect of your life and you can commence your heavenly experience while you are still here on earth. Follow Jesus to the gates of heaven. His willingness to lead us to glory will comfort us during our most difficult times. Riding His coat tails into heaven does not diminish our effort on this earth. Hold onto Him with all your might. Experience heaven and share God with others so that they may get a glimpse of heavenly glory. The joy-filled life can only lead to something better. Spice up this life with a little heaven; the rewards are infinite.

LESSON 20

The Least of Our Brothers

*Compassion is sometimes the fatal capacity
for feeling what it is like to live inside somebody else's skin.
It is the knowledge that there can never really be
any peace and joy for me until there is peace
and joy finally for you too.*

Frederick Buechner

Each day during the summer, I practice my daily ritual of packing for the beach in Breezy Point. I load my wagon and head off with my wife, Allison, and the kids. I am usually able to fit all of our beach supplies into the wagon, so that Allison or the children do not have to worry about carrying anything. One day a few years ago as I was pulling the wagon through the sand, Allison suddenly ran to help a young girl who struggled pulling her cooler through the sand. When she returned a few moments later, I asked her what prompted her to help the girl. Allison responded, "I am always afraid that the person in need is Jesus and I don't want to neglect Him." "Oh, okay," I responded without a reaction, but I was blown away by her deep reflection. For those who do not know my wife, she is not a "holy roller." She is a kind and caring woman who always looks out for the good of others. She does not spout theological and philosophical gems on a daily basis. She usually leaves the articulation of the faith to me because I am "in the business." So when she nonchalantly summed up the teaching of Jesus in one instant, I was stunned. Perhaps, it was the earnest expression on her face that will stay with me for the rest of my life. Over and over, the passage from the Gospel of Matthew ran through my head:

> "For I was hungry, and you gave Me something to eat; I was thirsty, and you gave Me something to drink; I was a stranger, and you invited Me in; naked, and you clothed Me; I was sick, and you visited Me; I was in prison, and you came to Me." Then the righteous will answer Him, "Lord, when did we see You hungry, and feed You, or thirsty, and give You something to drink? And when did we see You a stranger, and invite You in, or naked, and clothe You? When did we see You sick, or in prison, and come to You?" The King will answer and say to them, "Truly I say to you, to the extent that you did it to one of these brothers of Mine, even the least of them, you did it to Me." (Matthew 25:35-40)

I contemplated this story as I prepared to write this chapter. I drove home from school thinking about how Allison's actions and words impressed me. As I sat at a red light, I watched an elderly woman trying to help her husband climb onto the curb from their car. Weakened from age, she was unable to raise his legs high enough for him to gain his balance. When the struggling couple caught my attention, the words of my wife echoed in my head, "Could it be Jesus?" I even questioned, "Is this some kind of test?" As I pondered those questions, the man started to fall slowly. Without any more thought, I ran from my car and caught him as he braced himself on a nearby garbage can. I lifted him to the curb and the couple proceeded on their way as if this happened every day. Perhaps, it did.

When I returned to my car, I couldn't help but be reminded again of Allison's words. Thinking of everyone we encounter as Jesus made me act differently. I didn't hesitate. I didn't assume that someone else would bear the burden. I wanted to do this myself. Jesus calls every one of us to spring into action. You can't score from the sidelines.

Earlier in the book, we spoke about how we need to reach out to others who have been rejected by the "in crowd." During His ministry, Jesus also demonstrated the importance of having compassion on those who suffered.

> A leper came to Him and kneeling down begged Him and said, "If you wish, you can make me clean." Moved with pity, He stretched out His hand and touched him and said to him, "I do will it. Be made clean." The leprosy left him immediately and he was made clean.
> (Mk 1:40-42)

He clearly showed those around Him that we will be judged on how we reach out to these people. Whether Jesus met the blind, the demonized, the mourning, the hungry or the ailing, He took the time to stop and help in any way He could. He never turned anyone away. Compassion calls us to "suffer with another." Our attitude must change from "It's all about me" to "It's all about you." St. Paul in his Letter to the Romans (12:15) reminds us that it is our duty as Christians to "rejoice with those who rejoice and weep with those who weep." Others will learn compassion if we practice it ourselves.

At Kellenberg Memorial High School, Advent and Lent are opportunities for our school community to assist others in need. We hold a drive for a special cause. We have provided clothing for the homeless. We have assisted unwed mothers struggling to care for their children. We have renovated homes for families in need. We have collected canned goods for food pantries. The goal of these drives has been not only to care for those who need our help, but to teach our students the importance of compassion. We spend our religion classes teaching our students about Jesus Christ and the Catholic faith, but without compassion and action these lessons would be empty. We need to put our faith into action. We can't pass by another in need. To understand Jesus is to see what He would have done for the person who is suffering.

Our culture spends so much time focusing on the misery of others. The nightly news and the evening tabloid shows herald the message of another divorce, arrest, house fire, tornado or another man-made or natural disaster. We might sigh and say, "Thank God, it's not me." However, the compassionate voice of Christ urges us to move into action. He wants our response to be, "What can *I* do to help?" Jesus the Master wants us to learn the art of compassion. His desire for us to look around and help others in need is unending. Open your eyes and you will find people suffering in your midst. Allow compassion to make you fully human. Let mercy show how to truly love. Put your heart in the place of another. Try on someone else's shoes. Walk with them as they suffer. Dry their tears with your compassion. Seek the heart of the Master and change the world around you.

Final Thoughts from the Master

Before the Master left the apostles, He gave them their final instructions. Before major exams, students always want to review the course material one last time. As a teacher your greatest hope is that the material you taught will stay with your students beyond the final exams. Hopefully this recap will not serve only as an overview of the Master's lessons, but also as a reference guide as to what each chapter has covered.

The Master wants us to remember these important themes:

1. True discipleship begins with an invitation from the Master. He knocks and awaits our answer. Each of us is invited in our own way. It is up to us to open the door; no one else can do this for us. Stop procrastinating. Go to Him.

2. Forgiving others helps us to deepen all of our relationships, not just where someone has done wrong against us. Forgiveness eases our burdens and lifts a heavy heart. Anger and resentment hurt us far more than others. Use the mercy of forgiveness to repair broken relationships. Remember the Master told us that we shall only be forgiven if we are willing to forgive others.

3. Open up those exclusive social circles to include the lonely and forgotten. Stop judging the book by its cover. Our inclination to prejudge may keep us from getting to know others. Reach out to those who have been left out by others. A kind word or an invitation can change loneliness and despair into confidence and self-satisfaction. No one wants to be alone. Be Christ's hand and extend it in love.

4. Honor your parents and work on all of your familial relationships. Your parents have given you the gift of life and shared their love with you since your conception. Cherish these relationships. Respect their guidance and mentoring. Learn from their devotion to Jesus. Reciprocate the sacrifices they have made for you, especially as they age and must depend on others.

5. Relying on material possessions leaves us empty and unfulfilled. Love the people in your life, not the objects. Don't buy into what our culture tells you will make you happy. Too many people worship material things rather than God. Trim the fat in your life. Less is more. Find the beauty of a simple and spiritual existence. Once we separate ourselves from our toys, we can become closer to the kingdom of heaven.

6. Lighten up! Stop taking life so seriously. A person who can laugh at themselves will find true joy. The Master wants us to be happy. Discover a sense of humor. Live with the heart of a child. Don't allow the responsibilities of adulthood to deprive you of the joy that God has given you. Look in the mirror and love the real you. Push aside the inhibitions that drag you down. Live, love and laugh!

7. Sexuality is a gift from God. Incorporate love into your attraction and sexual temptation will diminish. Living a chaste life will bring you into communion with God and others in a very special way. Lust tempts us to treat others as objects. Treat the human body as a temple constructed by God to be a place of worship. Become a lover, a lover of chastity.

8. Become a spiritual leader. When we take on the attributes of the Good Shepherd, we lead others to God and righteousness. There are many people who have lost their faith and gone astray. Bring them home. A true shepherd sacrifices himself for the good of the flock. People notice what you say and do. Lead by example and show them what the Master has done for them.

9. Live truth and show others the truth. In our world of relativism, each opinion is looked upon as being as good as the next. People ignore the objective truth. Seek the truth in every aspect of life. We can't make rules as we go along. Abide by the truth. Abide in Christ and you will know the truth.

10. Spread the peace of Christ in the world. There are people around us who do not recognize that faith in Jesus will bring about inner peace. Become the peacemaker. Help make sense out of restlessness and chaos. Resolve conflicts when they arise. Calm the hearts full of fear. Allow the peace of the Master to permeate your world.

11. Love as the Master loved. God created us to love and to be loved. Love makes us fully human. True love conquers selfishness and sin. Give yourself to others in love and become rich beyond belief. Follow the example of Jesus on the road to Calvary and discover true love. When we learn to love, we find communion with God and others.

12. Prayer is a key component in our relationship with God. No relationship can survive without communication. Bring your cares and worries to the Lord. Unburden your heart through prayer. Look at the Gospels and see how the Master prayed. Seek consolation through your conversation with God. Never hesitate to call upon Him.

13. "The last shall be first and the first shall be last." Seek the humility of the Master in the role you play in this life. Meekness calls us to put others ahead of ourselves. Be humble! People will recognize your talent and dedication when you put your heart into your work.

14. Emulate Christ the teacher. Teach people about the benefits of having a personal relationship with God. You can transform the world when you immerse others into an atmosphere of faith. The lessons surrounding Jesus are endless, since He Himself is infinite. Incorporate the Master into every teachable moment. Join the Master in the noblest profession, no matter what you do for a living.

15. Recognize the importance of God in your life. Jesus is the vine and we are the branches. We can't live without Him. Our lives must revolve around God. Prosperity can distract us from our relationship with God. The Master reminds us to put our trust in Him. He will never let us down.

16. Friendship with Christ knows no bounds or limits. As we examine how Jesus treated His friends, we understand how we should act in our own relationships. The Master shows that His friendship extends to all humanity. He desires to have an intimate relationship with us. As your best friend, Jesus will carry you when your burdens become too many.

17. Jesus gives us His greatest gift in the Eucharist. We must take advantage of this gift. Through Holy Communion, we enter into a special bond with Jesus. We should receive Him as often as we can. Mass should become a priority in our lives. Invite those around you to sit at His table and become one with Him.

18. Learn from the wisdom of Jesus the carpenter. His time in Nazareth was well spent. Each day in the carpenter's shop taught Him something new about life. Practice His patience. Stand back and look at the big picture. Remember that everything we do is of consequence. Create a beautiful life even though you may experience moments of pain.

19. A relationship with Jesus points us to His heavenly realm. We need Jesus if we are to enter the kingdom of heaven. Be a living example of His love in the world. Make no excuses for your faith. Keep your mind focused on things above rather than those on earth. Begin your heavenly existence now.

20. Practice compassion. The Master constantly tells His followers that the way we treat others will determine whether or not we will gain entrance into His heavenly kingdom. Walk in another's shoes to understand how they feel. Comfort the weary and dry the tears of the grieving. Reach out to the suffering as Jesus did.

Jesus desires happiness and fulfillment for each of us. As He spoke with authority, the people started to refer to Him as the Master. They gravitated to Jesus because of His unique message. The Master's message was radical. Instead of revenge, He preached forgiveness. Knowing we are limited by sin and death, He spoke about redemption and eternal life. Consult with Him as you consider each move that you make. Follow His example and discover profound joy. Keep Him in your heart and unveil true love. Seek His wisdom, His experience, and His infinite knowledge. May His gentle hand guide you always as you walk beside Him.

Questions for Reflection and Discussion

Lesson One – The Invitation

1. How have you responded to the invitation from Jesus?
2. Have you invited others to follow Him?
3. Why are others so resistant to accept His invitation?

Lesson Two – Turn the Other Cheek

1. Who do you need to forgive in your life?
2. What is keeping you from forgiving them?
3. Reflect on the times that people have forgiven you.
4. For what do you need people to forgive you?

Lesson Three – The Outstretched Hand

1. Reflect on the people that you have neglected to invite into your social circle.
2. Why have you resisted inviting them to join you?
3. Have you ever felt neglected?
4. How has an invitation changed your life?

Lesson Four – The Faithful Son

1. What are some of the conflicts that you have with your parents?
2. How could you become a better son or daughter?
3. Reflect on Jesus' time in Nazareth. How does His dedication inspire you to be a better son or daughter?

Lesson Five – The Eye of the Needle

1. What are your most prized possessions?
2. Do your possessions keep you from following Christ?
3. Have you walked away from Jesus because of your reluctance to let go of your material possessions?

Lesson Six – A Be-Attitude

1. How often do you laugh? What makes you laugh?
2. When are you at your happiest?
3. What is your best quality?
4. What do you want to change about yourself?

Lesson Seven – The Body Beautiful

1. How do you treat members of the opposite sex?
2. What role does sexual desire play in your relationship with your boyfriend/girlfriend or your husband/wife?
3. How do you deal with the temptation of lust?
4. Does your sexuality bring you closer to God or push you away from Him?

Lesson Eight – Follow the Leader

1. Who are the leaders in your life? Are you a leader?
2. Who determines whether or not your family attends Mass?
3. Do you morally elevate the people around you or do you bring them down?
4. What are the opportunities where you bring Christ to others?

Lesson Nine – The Whole Truth

1. What are examples of relativism in your life?
2. How have you combated relativism?
3. What are some instances where you have been subjectively wrong in your life?
4. How does Jesus bring truth into your life?

Lesson Ten – Keeping the Peace

1. What are some of the conflicts in your life that need resolution?
2. What are the ways in which you resolve the conflicts around you?
3. How does Jesus bring peace into your life?
4. What do you need to find real peace?

Lesson Eleven – Love Your Neighbor

1. What is your definition of love?
2. How do you show the people in your life that you really love them?
3. When you reflect on the love of the cross, how can you bring that love into your life?

Lesson Twelve – Conversations with God

1. How often do you pray? What do you pray for?
2. Do you feel that your prayers are answered?
3. What distracts you from real prayer?
4. When and where can you best concentrate on communicating with God?

Lesson Thirteen – The Humble One

1. Who are the people who best exemplify the example Jesus showed His apostles at the Last Supper?
2. Where do you need more humility in your life?

3. Do you serve others?

4. How can you better serve them?

Lesson Fourteen – Caught, Not Taught

1. Who were your most influential teachers? What lessons did they teach you?

2. What lessons has Jesus taught you?

3. What life lessons do you feel that you share with others?

Lesson Fifteen – Lean on Me

1. What role does God play in your life?

2. What are the times in your life that you have felt that you did not need God?

3. How do you show your trust in God?

Lesson Sixteen – My Best Friend

1. Who is your best friend? What are their best qualities?

2. What would your friends say are your best qualities as a friend?

3. How are you a friend of Jesus? Would He consider you faithful? Why or why not?

Lesson Seventeen – Bread from Heaven

1. How often do you go to Mass and receive the Eucharist?

2. We often hear we become what we eat. Do we allow the Eucharistic presence of Jesus to transform who we are?

3. What do you reflect on or pray for after you receive Communion?

Lesson Eighteen – Measure Twice, Cut Once

1. What is the most beautiful thing that you have created?

2. Where do you need more patience in your life?

3. What have you learned from the Jesus the carpenter?

Lesson Nineteen – The Big Payoff

1. Do you believe in heaven? Describe what you think heaven will be like.
2. Do you pray to your friends and relatives in heaven?
3. How does the notion of heaven affect the way you live your life?

Lesson Twenty – The Least of Our Brothers

1. Where have you practiced compassion in your life?
2. When have others shown you compassion?

ST PAULS

This book was produced by ST PAULS/Alba House, the Society of St. Paul, an international religious congregation of priests and brothers dedicated to serving the Church through the communications media.

For information regarding this and associated ministries of the Pauline Family of Congregations, write to the Vocation Director, Society of St. Paul, 2187 Victory Blvd., Staten Island, New York 10314-6603. Phone (718) 982-5709; or E-mail: vocation@stpauls.us or check our internet site, www.vocationoffice.org